TRAIN WRECK

THE LIFE AND DEATH OF
ANNA NICOLE SMITH

BY
DONNA HOGAN

AS TOLD TO
HENRIETTA TIEFENTHALER

PHOENIX BOOKS

ISBN: 1-59777-540-1
Library of Congress Cataloging-In-Publication Data Available

Book Design by: Sonia Fiore

Printed in the United States of America

Phoenix Books
9465 Wilshire Boulevard, Suite 315
Beverly Hills, CA 90212

10 9 8 7 6 5 4 3 2 1

TABLE OF CONTENTS

INTRODUCTION

*"You can kid the world.
But not your sister."*
—CHARLOTTE GRAY

I am Anna Nicole Smith's half sister. I was born in 1971, four years after Vickie Lynn Hogan, whom you know as Anna Nicole Smith. In some ways we are very similar and perhaps that is why I can understand her motivations, but in other ways we are completely different.

In the years since my sister became famous I've gained a lot of notoriety—unwanted notoriety—mostly caused by a media fixated on my sister, but sometimes caused directly by Anna. My children and I have been ruthlessly stalked by paparazzi and other media types. Every time my sister did something, usually bizarre, the paparazzi hounded my work place as well as my house, hiding in the bushes and even on the roof of my home.

At times it's hard to sustain a career with all of that going on. They camp outside the door, taking pictures and asking all kinds of crazy questions. It's impossible to keep normal friends because the normal every day person doesn't want to put up with that. I mean, can you imagine going out with your girlfriends and trying to have a good time and then—boom! Out from nowhere comes someone with a camera the size of a truck. Imagine the U.S. tabloids and the U.K. newspapers are either ruthlessly snapping photo after photo or running you down with never-ending questions about some silly thing or other you have absolutely no clue about.

Then, there are the top-tier television shows like *Nancy Grace, Larry King Live, Good Morning America, The Today Show, The Early Show* and others who call for interviews and comments. I admire them all, but they only want me on their shows to talk about my crazy sister and her wacky life. It's hard to continually explain my sister's bizarre behavior on national television. My sister who dubbed me a "user-loser" and told the world the incredible lie that she had never even met me!

The bottom line is that I'm writing this because over the past decade there have been numerous lies about my family and me in the tabloids. I could have sold out many years ago, but I wanted, in my way, to protect Anna and keep some dignity. Despite being offered thousands and thousands of dollars for pictures and stories, I chose to stay quiet. I was struggling financially as a single mother, but I never took a dime. Instead we endured embarrassing misery with all her media stunts. It's her actions that brought the press to my door. At first we all thought she would be a flash in the pan and fade away, but over the years she managed to continually up her antics and stay front-page news.

But...I have my own life. I don't live and breathe Anna Nicole. By writing this book perhaps I can once and for all put some of the questions I get asked to rest. I am not perfect; I never claimed to be. I'm just trying to lead a decent life, take care of my three children and find answers to why my sister, my blood, treated us the way she did over these past years.

It has been a catharsis for me to write this book and perhaps by writing it I will be able to better understand who Vickie was. This is also a tale of two sisters who had dreams, whose lives intertwined, then fell apart, and lost each other. It's my turn to tell the true story! In doing so, however, be warned. I have strong opinions. When I see something or, after talking to my family, or my sister's family or people I trust, learn something, I can be very direct in telling it the way I see it. It's just my opinion. I know there may be two sides to the story, and I'm happy to hear the other side, just not necessarily in my book. If, in the end, my opinion is wrong, then I'll be the first to admit it and apologize for anyone who feels unfairly accused. But, until someone comes and proves me wrong, here it is....

DONNA HOGAN
MONTGOMERY COUNTY, TEXAS
MARCH 2007

PROLOGUE

*W*orking with Donna has been a roller coaster ride of its own. The tales she has shared with me are beyond anything I could ever have anticipated. Together, we have researched all perspectives of Anna's life in order to deliver to you, the public, her story. My only regret is that during the process of writing this book, our much-loved protagonist sadly passed away.

She was one of the most beautiful, yet larger than life, celebrities this country has ever witnessed. Hollywood screenwriters could not have brainstormed such a tale as the true-life story of Vickie Lynn Hogan, better known to the public as Anna Nicole Smith. This gorgeous, breathtaking sex symbol of the last two decades was admired by many and jeered by others. The public and the media both had a love-hate relationship with Anna Nicole Smith. What was the fascination with this complex woman? Why was the media coverage of her untimely death as massive worldwide as the coverage for the passing of a president or royalty? Why did America and the world care so much about the life and tragic death of Anna Nicole Smith?

To begin this story one has to look back at the beginning and how this Texas-born beauty, with a limited education and no money, struggled to make her way out of her small town and into the big time of Hollywood. Nothing would stop her; she was determined to be a star!

Anna was born in 1967. That year, *The Man For All Seasons* won the Academy Award, Frank Sinatra received a Grammy for *Strangers in the Night*, Congress created PBS, and *Rolling Stone* and *New York Magazine* debuted. On a more serious note, it was also the year that President Lyndon Johnson decided not to seek re-election because of the unpopular war in Vietnam and Thurgood Marshall was sworn in as the first black U.S. Supreme Court Justice.

Anna dropped out of school in the tenth grade, at the age of fifteen, to work at Jim's Krispy Fried Chicken as a waitress. That was followed by a stint as a cashier at Wal-Mart. In 1985, when she was only seventeen, she married her sweetheart, a fry cook, Billy Smith, and they had a baby boy shortly after. In 1986, she was hospitalized for a drug overdose and in 1987, she and Billy divorced.

Her career then took her to strip and perform under the name of "Miss Nikki" and "Robyn." As a stripper at Rick's Plaza, a gentlemen's club in Houston, she didn't hesitate to bump and grind for tough, wild audiences in nothing but a G-string. Later, Anna would act in a Paul Newman film, *The Hudsucker Proxy*; become a spokesperson for Guess? Jeans, replacing supermodel Claudia Schiffer, a "columnist" for the *National Enquirer*; star of her own reality show for A&E, *The Anna Nicole Show*. Most notoriously, at twenty-six she became the wife of eighty-nine-year-old oil billionaire J. Howard Marshall.

After cosmetic surgery and implants, she entered the *Playboy* Cover Contest and, at the age of twenty-four, she won. In May 1992, the dream continued when she was named Playmate of the Month and in 1993, she was crowned Playmate of the Year. These were amazing accomplishments for this small-town girl! Her family and friends were very proud of their local rising star!

Anna Nicole Smith was an exception to the starvelings who usually flaunted themselves in pages of *Playboy*—weighing in at one-hundred-and-forty pounds, partly accounted for by an expensively enhanced chest the size of Texas. However, Anna's path to stardom and financial security did not come without a price. She may have had a glamorous Hollywood existence, but tragedy always followed her. She was never in control of her life. Drugs, alcohol and controversy seemed to always take center stage.

Sadly on a path that would become all too familiar, in February 1994, she was admitted to Cedars Sinai hospital for yet another drug overdose, this time in a coma. She was admitted to the Betty Ford Clinic for rehab and charged with assault and sexual harassment by her former female lover. Her spending was also out of control and, in 1996, she filed for bankruptcy.

Ten years later, the drama in her life had by no means mellowed. In 2006, the media said that she was "The Biggest Hollywood Story of the Year" after the birth of her daughter, the tragedy of losing her son Daniel, whom she loved more than life itself, the paternity suits against her, being evicted from her ex-boyfriend's house in the Bahamas, her commitment ceremony to Howard K. Stern just weeks after her son's death, and the ongoing battle for her late husband's fortune.

Then, just five months after her son died as a result of the interaction of too many drugs, on February 8, 2007, her life tragically came to an end for apparently the same reason as her son's. Her death was a media phenomenon that could equal the media coverage received by Marilyn Monroe at her death in 1962. Marilyn Monroe was Anna's life-long idol. Since childhood, Anna told everybody she would be the next Marilyn Monroe and, in hindsight, she was partially right.

Anna had one of the most famous names and most famous faces in the Western world, with the British tabloids even more gaga over her than the U.S. media…if that's possible.

When a producer at the popular U.S. television news-magazine, *A Current Affair*, was asked why her program ran so many segments featuring the latest Anna Nicole antics, she replied, "She's a train wreck...and train wrecks draw viewers." People cannot stop themselves from being intrigued by her life. No matter how outlandish she may have seemed, Anna could always reinvent herself. She proved her ability to attract an audience by remaining in the spotlight for almost twenty years. The ratings of major interview shows such as *Entertainment Tonight, Access Hollywood*, E*!* and *The Tonight Show*, always jumped when she was on. She routinely drew more viewers than most A-list Hollywood actors.

Despite her lack of acting talent, Anna made it as a star. It is difficult to pinpoint what made Anna so different from every other aspiring wannabe. Was it her looks, her chest size, or her crazy antics? Anna Nicole had to resort to specially-made bras as her size became Double F's. She made frequent appearances in the pages of the tabloid newspapers: for an Anna Nicole story, they didn't have to make up lurid details, just reporting the truth was enough.

She walked around her house naked, not just as a little girl, but right through her teen years and even after getting married. At the end of the first episode of her reality show she told her television audience: "I didn't get to masturbate this morning, and I've been dying to, so I've gotta go." She was so out of control, either drunk or on drugs at a Live 8 concert, where she appeared as a presenter, that the charity filed a suit against her. And she hit the tabloid and TV headlines once again when she assaulted a staff member at the tony Beverly Hills Hotel.

But it's not just the tabloid press and the TV talk shows that knew they could draw attention with Anna Nicole. She was the subject of pieces in *Vanity Fair, Esquire, New York* magazine, *Los Angeles* magazine, and *TV Guide* (where at times her name popped up in almost every issue). Meanwhile, the prestigious business Internet site *Forbes.com* announced results of a survey to identify the ten most financially savvy people in America; at the top of the list were financier Warren Buffett, and then-Federal Reserve

Chairman Alan Greenspan, while in spot number five was—yes, Anna Nicole…ahead of Bill Gates and Donald Trump.

What earned her that place must have something to do with her unruly ten-year battle to obtain as much as $440 million from the estate left by the ninety-year-old, wheelchair-bound oil baron she was married to for thirteen months. When the case was heard by the U.S. Supreme Court last February, the frenetic cameramen crushing her were not the usual crowd of paparazzi. This unruly pack (one of whom got knocked to the ground by his own over-eager colleagues) was representing the likes of the major U.S. television networks, plus the BBC and CNN.

The lady was eminently quotable. About working in strip joints and posing naked for *Playboy*, she said, "I always used to think, 'Am I going to hell for this? God is not going to like this.'" But she was reassured because Adam and Eve were naked "and God loved their bodies. They never had clothes until she ate that stupid piece of [fruit]." Anna claimed she had never had plastic surgery, but the evidence shows that everything about her but her trademark Texas country twang was manufactured: her breasts, lips, teeth, and weight loss.

Even her name (she was born Vickie Lynn Hogan) was fabricated. She may have been a train wreck, but she was a train wreck people still can't seem to get enough of. The sordid but fascinating story of her vicious, no-holds-barred battle with life is one of the most gripping, sex-soaked biographies in years.

This is the story of a little girl from west of nowhere, who was born into a broken, dysfunctional, dirt-poor family; a mother at seventeen, facing a hardscrabble life, like many of her relatives. She developed a fierce resolve that allowed her to claw her way to celebrity status and the potential of great wealth. This is a Horatio Alger story with a dark side. It's also a story that is testimony to what sheer determination can achieve.

Anna's kid sister, co-author Donna Hogan, grew up in the same aching poverty, with a crazy mother, and a father who sexually abused her. Like Anna, she quit high school in tenth grade and started working at gentlemen's clubs. Their lives took a similar path, as both Anna and Donna worked in clubs and both took too many prescription drugs, and lived a wild, unfettered life. Donna stopped, but Anna continued on that destructive path.

Anna Nicole has been labeled one of the stupidest women on the face of the earth and Mr. Blackwell's number one worst dressed woman in America. Larry Flynt may have summed her up the best: "How many bimbos with nothing get to marry a billionaire?" She may not have been so "stupid" but rather carefully crafted the image she wanted to portray.

However, this is a tale full of contradictions. Anna was ridiculed and vilified, yet given her own national TV series. At times, she was demeaned and laughed at, yet the Bush administration sent its top lawyer to file a brief on her behalf in her fight for her late husband's mega millions. She was teetering on the brink of inheriting $87 million, or maybe as much as $440 million, but she declared bankruptcy. She gave the impression of being an irresponsible sex queen, but managed to raise a bright, gentle son who loved her.

While Anna Nicole collected big money as the spokes-woman for a diet pill she insisted slimmed her from dowdy to supermodel-thin, Donna has evidence to support her claim that Anna's real route to skinniness consisted of drugs, surgery and Slimfast shakes.

So much of this story will read like fiction, but then, the truth about Anna Nicole is stranger than any novel ever could be. Donna writes about Anna Nicole from her unique perspective as her half-sister, and with the benefit of access to many who knew Anna throughout her life, first in Houston and later in the dusty, wind-swept town of Mexia, Texas, including Anna's mother Virgie, Anna's troubled first husband Billy, Anna's childhood friends, ex-publicist, co-stars, and other relatives. Even though they had been estranged for the past ten years and Donna did not agree with many of Anna's choices in life, she loved and admired her big sister for what she had achieved. Yet she always felt a deep concern for her health and well-being.

Anna Nicole made many Hollywood friends and just as many enemies in her climb to the top and she has created a large pool of people who will share their stories. The group includes ex-employees (bodyguards like Pierre DeJean, housekeepers like the Hispanic maid whose lawsuit led to Anna's bankruptcy) and service providers (hairdressers, fitness trainers and J. Howard Marshall's nurse Letitia Hunt, who knows the truth about how Anna behaved with her billionaire husband). The list goes on: attorneys like Don Jackson and Rusty Hardin (who represented Marshall's son Pierce in the inheritance dispute) and ex-lovers of which there have been many—including Sandi Powledge, one of the lesbian girlfriends, and Clay Spires, a bed-pal while Anna was dating J. Howard and after she married him.

Happily there's a rosy side to the story, as well. Many of the people she worked with professionally tell of a different kind of woman. Sure, a small-town Texas girl with an attitude, but also a hard-working woman who was determined to be a celebrity and a success no matter what anyone thought.

The PETA organization felt she was one of their best spokespersons in their fight against animal cruelty in the history of their organization. Anna was a friend to animals and always doted on her eccentric array of pets.

She impacted everyone along her road to stardom: from the people at *Playboy* who ran the nude pictures she herself sent in, to the Guess? clothing company executives, to the product managers who chose her to enrich their company coffers, to the Hollywood producers and directors such as Mark Juris (*N.Y.U.K.*) and feature film director Peter Segal (*Naked Gun 33 1/3*), to Mark McDermott, Darren Ewing, and Kevin Hayes, the producers of her TV reality series. They all shaped her talents to their needs. She made entire creative teams happy, despite occasionally driving them crazy. Even her baby sister Donna says, "Despite growing up in a family where no big dreams come true, she succeeded at something and fought her way to the top, no matter what anybody else thought."

Unfortunately, Anna's fierce resolve was just a façade. She may not have appeared to care what others thought of her outlandish ways but deep down she was never truly happy with herself. Anna's life was a rollercoaster ride; a constant battle with drugs, weight, and a ravenous hunger for fame. Ultimately she lost the fight and the train crashed to its fatal end.

HENRIETTA TIEFENTHALER
HOLLYWOOD, CALIFORNIA
MARCH 2007

CHAPTER 1

VICKIE LYNN HOGAN

> *"I knew I belonged to the public
> and to the world, not because
> I was talented or even beautiful,
> but because I had never belonged
> to anything or anyone else."*
> —MARILYN MONROE

Anna Nicole Smith was born as Vickie Lynn Hogan on November 28, 1967, in Houston, Texas, to a father, Donald Eugene Hogan, who abused the people who should have been near and dear to him, and a mother who she felt resented her.

Anna's mother, Virgie Mae Tabers, was married to Anna's (and my) father, Donald Hogan, for only a few years. Donald moved out of the house after Vickie was born, and the marriage was cut short when Vickie was two because of Dad's alleged abuse of Virgie and Virgie's sister, Aunt Kay. Donald Hogan was accused of statutory rape of Virgie's ten-year-old sister, Kay, and of another underage girl. After pleading guilty, he spent six months in jail, and then got off with a ten-year probation. He was also accused of beating and mentally abusing Virgie, even while she was pregnant with Anna. He often beat the kids in my family, including me, and had a long history of violent behavior. Our father was an alcoholic.

Back then if you were a convicted sex offender, you did not have to register with the National Sex Offender Public Registry. This has since been created so that if you look any sex offender up on the list, their name will be displayed. It also enables everyone in the neighborhood to be alerted when a sex offender is moving into the area. When Donald was charged, the list did not exist and his name has never been put on the Registry. Although, thinking back, even if his name had been on a registry, my mom would probably still have married him—she always was attracted to trouble.

My mother, Wanda, was married to our dad, Donald Hogan, until their divorce when I was seven years old. They remained in an on-and-off relationship throughout the years, which was very awkward for me. They even tried to make their relationship work again, years later, when Anna decided to reunite with our family.

When Anna started making a name for herself she momentarily decided to have our father's side of the family back in her life. At this point my parents attempted to play happy family, but it was in vain. My mother is a nut and my father has the ability to destroy everything around him so their personalities did not make the best combination for a thriving relationship.

I am the eldest of my mother's five children. Wanda is completely psychotic and mal-treated all of her children. In recent years, Wanda has been institutionalized numerous times and has been clinically diagnosed with severe delusion. I committed her to a mental asylum three years ago, but she got out after a few months and then, a year and a half ago, she was sent back in again.

My mother has gotten worse over the years. At times, she claims Hitler is her father and believes that her children were implanted in her. She has accused all of us of not being hers and she has called me the Devil on numerous occasions.

Wanda was always abusive to me and would always be attracted to men who treated her badly and sexually molested her children. I had a really disturbing upbringing, but I felt I had to stick around in order to protect my younger siblings. I did not leave home until I was eighteen years old.

Every day of our childhood we would be attacked both verbally and physically. Even when I was as young as seven years old, she would scream at me and call me a whore and a slut, accusing me of trying to steal her boyfriends. Instead of protecting me from her abusive lovers, she would accuse me of coming on to them. As a result, I was so jaded by men, I did not have my first boyfriend until I was nineteen years old.

Instead of leading a normal teenage life, I sacrificed having fun so that I could take care of my younger brothers and sisters. I was the mother figure in our household. Wanda was always away so I had to cook and clean and look after the others. We were happy when she left because it meant that we could get on with our lives instead of being beaten and screamed at.

Once I made spaghetti for everyone to eat because there was no other food around. My mother beat me with a belt for not making anything to go with it. The buckle cut across my face as well as other parts of my body, leaving scratches and deep-set red marks on my skin. She continued to abuse me incessantly as long as she had more power over me. But once I grew bigger than her and could fight back, she attacked me less.

We were always shoved here and there for long periods of time. The longest was when I was between the ages of seven and eight. My younger brother and sister, Donnie and Amy, and I were sent to live with our grandparents for a year because Wanda did not want to look after her children. While we were there, our mother went to live with another man, Lloyd Wayne Elmor. He was already living with his long-term girlfriend so the three of them lived together in the same house: my mother, her boyfriend and his other girlfriend.

She conceived twins with this guy and wanted him to leave his other girlfriend. After he refused, she moved out and married someone else, while still pregnant. Wayne has never acknowledged his children, even after they tried to contact him years later.

I was nine years old when the twins, Larry and Jerry, were born. They lived with us too, so that added two more siblings for me to look after. I was the one who had to change their diapers and feed them. There were five of us by then and I took on the responsibility for all of them. No one believed that I would ever want children after everything I had to endure.

I did have children later, but I vowed never to tell them about any of the horrible details of my upbringing. I have always tried to make sure that they were surrounded by stable people and, if anyone were even to mention abuse, I would make certain that my children were removed from it. I have tried to distance myself from the violence that I was a victim of and put it behind me—after all, I have seen the effects that an upbringing like mine can have on people. You can too, if you just look at the lives of Anna and our sister, Amy.

Amy was born in Texas in 1975. She has the same vocational aspirations as Anna. She too craves the limelight and would do anything to reach celebrity status. Amy did not meet Anna because they could not even manage to get along over the phone. Amy and Anna couldn't stand each other up until the very end. They had very similar personalities, clashing and competing to be the center of attention. On the phone, Amy would be vindictive towards our sister, probably out of jealousy, and Anna would just hang up. She wouldn't take shit from anyone if she didn't have to.

Amy doesn't resemble the Hogan gene as much as Anna and I, and sometimes our dad questions whether she is even his, probably just to get out of paying child support. Donald and Wanda split up for two months around the time Amy was conceived and Donald claimed that she couldn't have been his.

However, my mother insists she was pregnant with Amy before they had split. Anna enjoyed telling people she and Amy weren't related.

Amy turned into a serious drug addict at a young age and ended up having her three boys taken away from her. She met her future second husband, Chris, while scoring drugs; he was the local drug dealer.

Sometimes when we were all sitting around together, her kids would brag to us that Chris had taught them how to break into people's houses. Amy thought it was cute and the boys thought it was funny, but the rest of us were shocked. Larry, one of our twin brothers, got really angry. He was staying with them at the time, but soon after he moved out.

When Larry later came and lived with me, I found out that Amy and Chris were doing drugs in front of her kids. Once, her eldest son, Andrew, had asked Larry if he had a bump on him. Larry was furious that his nephew had tried to score drugs off him.

Amy was not feeding her boys as she spent all her money on drugs. They were renting their apartment and, at one point, when desperate for money, sold the fridge and the stove even though it didn't belong to them. The only thing that was left was an ice chest for the kids to eat on. The landlord pressed charges and Chris got arrested. He already had a warrant on him for a theft that he had been accused of, but the police hadn't found enough evidence against him to convict.

Larry and I couldn't bear the way Amy's boys were being brought up, so we called the police. We had all had a miserable childhood, living under our mother's roof while she took drugs. We had always said that if one of us turned out to be like our parents, another had to step in, and so Larry and I felt it was our duty to report Amy. When Amy found out it was me who reported her, she threatened to have me "whacked off."

The police went over to her house and the situation there was plain to see. With drugs lying around all over the place and no food or furniture, they immediately called Child Protection Services (CPS). The police questioned the neighbors, who revealed that Amy's boys often came knocking for food and money, and they had seen Amy and Chris doing drugs outside in the open.

When the police called CPS, it was after hours and there was no one available. They gave Amy a court date, during which all the information would be evaluated, and then left. One of the police officers on duty was an old boyfriend of Amy's and he told the other officers that he would make sure the kids were fed and that she attended court, so they let her off easy.

Amy, Chris and the kids skipped town and didn't show up at court. That meant her rights were immediately terminated and the children were illegally under her care. It turned out that CPS had been called about Amy before—Larry and I were obviously not the only people concerned for her children. Amy was difficult to track down, especially after she knew the cops were looking for her. From 2004 to mid-2006, they all lived in homeless shelters in Texas and out of state.

Following in her mother's footsteps, Amy married Chris, a man who took drugs and abused her. They married because the homeless shelter forbade men and women from sleeping in the same room unless they were married. Amy fell pregnant with Chris's daughter while they were living at the homeless shelter. In 2004, Amy gave birth and, unfortunately, although CPS eventually caught up with her and took away the boys, she ended up getting custody of their daughter.

As well as being pot smokers, they had a methamphetamine addiction. I have witnessed their paranoia from the drugs. At times, they thought they were seeing aliens and that everyone was an FBI agent looking for them. With our mother Wanda's history of mental illness, I am afraid that Amy is going in that direction, too. Wanda was also a drug addict and sometimes I am not sure whether it was her mental condition or the drugs that landed her in an asylum.

When she was on drugs, Amy had no sense of what was going on around her and completely abandoned her kids. The neighbors once found one of her sons freezing outside in a diaper and none of the boys went to school for almost an entire year.

Before the children got taken away, Amy took her family to stay with our younger brother, Donnie, who lived down the street from our dad in Oakhurst, Texas. The place was derelict and no one was supposed to be living in it, but Donnie, Amy and her family squatted the building. When they first moved in, the windows were broken and the children froze, especially at night. The place didn't even have running water. They would have to go down the street to our dad's place to use the shower and wash the dishes. Dad hated having them all in his house. He didn't trust Chris because he knew that he stole. Chris also had a bad vibe about him that everyone could sense when they met him. He was always jittery and made racist comments, which really upset me. His family is Hispanic but he denies it, adamant that he is a supremacist.

Chris's ex-girlfriend, Deonna, is a friend of mine. Way back, before Amy dated Chris, Deonna and I were roommates. During that time, she got together with Chris and had a kid with him. While they were living together, Amy and I would sometimes go over and visit. Amy always spoke badly about Chris and his drug habit; she couldn't understand what Deonna saw in him. Less than ten years later she ended up stealing him off Deonna and marrying him. I am still friends with Deonna and so I know when Chris has a job because she tells me when she has received a bit of the child support he owes.

When CPS tracked Amy down, she gave custody of her sons to their fathers. Andrew and Timmy were sent to live with Jim, in Wyoming, and Taylor was sent to his dad, Tom, in Montana.

When Amy was pregnant with her first child, Taylor, she was secretly taking crack with a friend of hers. She did it behind

Tom's back and when the baby was born a "crack baby" it came as a shock to all of us. Tom was against drugs and, except for smoking a bit of pot now and then, he didn't touch them. Taylor was born in Billings, Montana, and Amy was not allowed to immediately hold him. He had to be taken away to another hospital to be weaned off the drugs.

Once Amy was awarded custody of Taylor, she had to be supervised twice a day for months. CPS would be in her house to evaluate how she was as a mother, so that put an end to her crack habit.

After Amy left Tom for Chris, he was devastated. Even when Alexis, her baby with Chris, was born, Tom offered to take her back; he was still in love. Since then, Tom has become an alcoholic and, although he was awarded custody of his son, Taylor gets sent back and forth between parents. When Tom can't take being a father any more, he ships the boy back to his drug-addict mother. For some reason, Amy is allowed to have her other sons on weekends now too.

Considering our background, I have always thought that Vickie drew the lucky straw. Her mother, Virgie, made sure that our abusive father, Donald Hogan, was never allowed to lay a finger on her and, despite what Vickie said, Virgie made sure her daughter grew up in a middle-class household.

I truly respect Virgie for keeping Vickie away from our father as there is no doubt that, given the chance, he would have abused her too. He abused all the other women in his life, including me, his own daughter—Anna was lucky to have escaped that trauma.

Abuse is very difficult to deal with on any level and certainly served to drive a wedge among our family members. Virgie's deep hatred towards Donald and anything to do with him grew to become interminable. She has done everything in her power to avoid me, and everyone else related to Donald. No matter how hard I have tried to communicate with her, she does not want to have anything to do with me.

Vickie grew up thinking that that her mother hated her and was punishing her for being Donald's daughter. This deeply affected her and she would sneak out of the house to try to find him. Once Virgie found out that Vickie was associating with her father, she refused to have any contact with Vickie. She was very upset that her own daughter had gone behind her back to seek out Donald, especially after everything that she had told Vickie about him. Donald's bad karma had a ripple effect on everyone he touched, but Vickie was oblivious to any of his faults. Only later would she come to realize what he was really like.

Vickie lived in a little wooden house on Brenda Street, Houston, with Virgie and her stepfather, another Donald (his last name was Hart). He brought two children he had had from a previous marriage into the family: his daughter, Shauna, and son, Robert. Vickie could never stand her stepsister, Shauna. She probably saw the other girl in the house as competition. Shauna was always the mother hen and bossed Anna around because she was older. She would also try to get Anna into trouble with her mother. Shauna has since married a multi-millionaire and is richer than Anna was, and Anna really couldn't stand that. The saddest thing about Anna's hostility toward her is that Shauna contracted leukemia and became very ill, and Anna still wouldn't speak to her.

Virgie had also previously had a child. She had married a Mr. Tacker at about fourteen or fifteen years of age and they had a son, David, who is now an FBI agent. After she divorced our father, Virgie married Donald Hart and they had a child together, whom they called Donald Hart, Jr., Dino for short.

Virgie and Donald Hart were very disciplined and religious. They believed in strong family values, which Anna rebelled against. The couple maintained a stable family environment; they raised all five of their children under one roof and didn't divorce until all of them had grown up.

Linda Compton-Dove went to Northline elementary school with Anna. They studied together in Mr. Yawn's class in sixth grade and became friends immediately. Linda lived with her grandma who would often drop Anna home after school, but Anna was rarely allowed to go out. Sometimes, Linda would hang out at Anna's house. She says Virgie was really strict and made her stay home and do the chores. Virgie drove a baby blue little Volkswagen with tinted tree scenes on it. Anna hated the car. Linda eventually moved away to live with her parents and the two friends drifted apart.

They became friends once more in ninth grade as they were again in the same class at Aldine High School in Houston. Anna had moved to Connorvale Street in the Aldine Imperial Valley area. Linda says that Anna was a really kind person to be with. Her soft-spoken voice was so cute and it often got her out of trouble with the teachers.

Anna hooked up with her brother David's best friend, John, but it was nothing serious. The boys were all part of a gang that included David, John, Chuck, and Lee. Linda ended up marrying Lee for twenty years, but then they divorced. The boys were terrors. They would do everything together and cause havoc.

Unlike what Anna has told the media about her family—that we are *all* "white trash"—many of us are professionals, such as small business owners, nurses and police officers. No matter what her claims are, Vickie had a comparatively easy life as a child and I have always been envious of her family situation.

Despite the demeaning comments about her relatives, until her billionaire husband, J. Howard Marshall, died, she always wanted us around her. Virgie and David were even in two of her movies, *To the Limit* and *Skyscraper*, but after J. Howard's death Anna distanced herself from all her relatives. She thought we would be after his money if she were to win the court battle for his estate, and so excommunicated all of us. This was also around the time that Howard K. Stern was introduced onto the scene. I cannot help but think that he had a large role in Anna's abrupt alienation from everybody around her, other than her son.

The Hogan family was always supportive of Anna, especially in her early years and when she first hit Hollywood. Although Virgie refused to have anything to do with us Hogans, we were always there for her daughter when she needed us. During these initial years, we would be at her beck and call, but she considered her family to be dispensable; when she was doing well she wanted nothing to do with us.

Vickie said that her mom always abused her, which is why she left home at sixteen. Even though her father was forced out of the home and barred by a restraining order for the abuse of his wife and children, as a child Vickie kept trying to locate him. She would search for his name in the phone book, even though she knew she would be punished by her mother for the attempt. Virgie did not want Vickie looking for her dad and was very upset when Vickie tried to find him.

I remember as a little girl my dad and mom would drive us by Vickie's home. My dad would say, "Look Donna, there is your big sister." And I would see this child swinging on her swing set. It's funny though, because back then she had dark hair and I remember my first response being, "Why does she have dark hair when mine's blonde?" I didn't immediately recognize the fact that she was my sister.

It seemed so tranquil and pretty at her house. I desperately wanted to jump out of the car and run to her and ask if we could be together, if I could come and live with her there. Her life looked so much better than mine. She lived on this farm-type home and I was envious of her swing set and garden.

I wanted my big sister in my life so bad, but my dad would tell me that I was not allowed to talk to her because Virgie would not allow it; I did not know the reasoning behind this at the time. He would then drive away as I looked out at my sister through the back window.

It's sad to think that I would be fantasizing about being with my big sister while she was so desperate to find her father, and we were all within such close proximity to one another. I guess the grass is always greener on the other side.

Vickie's mom became a police officer after she left our dad. However, two years ago a brain aneurysm cut her career short. She was in a coma for three months and had to learn to walk, talk and feed herself all over again. At the time, Vickie was already not speaking to her mother and would not allow any of the family to see her son, Daniel. Since their feud, Virgie has always said that all she wanted to do was to see her grandson. Although that didn't happen, in November 2005, I did find myself in a position to help Vickie's mom attempt a meeting with Daniel.

A syndicated television show was going to make it happen. I had pulled some strings and they agreed to unite her with Daniel. They would have organized and paid for their reunion, but Virgie refused to do the show because it wasn't paying her big money. She wanted to be paid upwards of $20,000 for her interview and refused to participate in the deal unless her price was met. They were offering her a fair amount, but she said it would be her first interview and they should be giving her more. Now, for all the money in the world, Virgie will never be able to see her grandson again.

I have since seen Virgie on almost every television station and you know what's funny? She has blonde hair too. The red-haired lady would always get on Vickie and me about our blonde hair and then she went and bleached her own hair. It's ironic because, although they would never admit it, in some ways, Virgie and her daughter are very similar.

They both knew what they wanted and would go to all lengths to get it. Money was very important to both mother and daughter, and it has led to a lot of tragedy in their lives. Money was the main reason that Anna stopped speaking to most of her family and it is the main reason that Virgie decided to publicly speak out against her daughter. Although they went about it differently, Virgie and Anna really wanted to be good parents but, in both cases, their children ended up suffering. Anna did anything for attention and Daniel would always shy away from the camera. Both children took to drugs as a form of escapism and eventually it killed them.

In adolescence, when other girls were filling out, Vickie, to her continuing dismay, remained flat-chested, with dark brown hair and a mannish look. She wasn't getting any affection at home and so she sought it elsewhere. She hungered for the attention of boys and was always jealous of other girls who got it, until she found that if she was wild enough, sexy enough, and loose enough, the boys would accept her company.

She began sneaking out of the house to hang with the wild crowd—the boys living on the edge—doing whatever you could imagine. Vickie continued to hang around these people even when the guys got angry and hit her. She proved to be open to whatever they wanted to do. She always went for the wrong men; the type who took drugs and drank excessively and would take their aggression out on her. It didn't take long for her to do the drugs with them, probably as a way to numb everything that was happening to her. It got to the point where she was totally out of control. According to her stepfather, Donald Hart, "She snuck out of the house with an older man and went off with him and got caught by her mother." That is when she got shipped off to Mexia, Texas.

Virgie was by then a police officer, but she couldn't discipline her wild and rebellious daughter. Desperate, Virgie shipped Vickie off to live with her sister, Kay Heard, in a village near Beverly Hills—not the luxurious California community but Beverly Hills, Texas (yes, there really is a Texas town with that name). A hardscrabble, dirt-poor place called Mexia (pronounced muh-HEY-uh). Once a thriving oil town with 7000 inhabitants, it is "a place to grow up and a place to retire to, but there's no middle there."

Vickie moved in with Aunt Kay, her cousins, Melinda and Shelly, and her uncle, Floyd Harrison, in a deteriorating white shack—enough to give any girl with dreams a lousy attitude and a sense of desperation. As a teenager, there was nothing for Vickie to do in Mexia. According to Melinda, "You have to go to Waco to do practically anything. [In Waco] there's a movie theater and bowling alley and skating rink, but there's not really much to do here [in Mexia]."

Her aunt was like a mother to her. She would call Kay "momma" and address Virgie as "mother." She told people that Virgie was not her real mother, explaining that her Aunt Kay had been raped by her father, had become pregnant with her and that she had been given to Virgie to bring up. Vickie compensated for the excitement that was lacking in her life, by making it up. She also vehemently insisted that Marilyn Monroe was her real mother, even though she had died five years before Vickie was born. There is no way Kay could be her mother either; she was only a ten-year-old girl when Donald had raped her.

Recently Anna's family was interviewed for an unauthorized documentary called *Dark Roots*. Once you see that footage you can truly fathom where Anna Nicole comes from. If you look at her relatives you can only admire Anna for getting out of Mexia. Judging by them, there is nothing to do there other than take drugs and eat greasy food. On camera, her uncle Floyd is chewing off his mouth, his jaw is sunken and he has lost his teeth. He is barely comprehensible and unhealthily skinny. He and his toothless daughter, Shelly, show all the signs of being methamphetamine addicts. Kay and their other daughter, Melinda, are the exact opposite. They are both heavily overweight and, judging by the amount of pharmaceutical bottles scattered around the house, we can see that Kay, if not Melinda as well, is drugged up on an assortment of prescription pills.

Vickie attended Mexia High School, but she did not have many friends. She would boast to the girls that, if she wanted to, she could take their boyfriends away from them and so they grew to hate her. Her decision to drop out of high school before she reached tenth grade, she later said, was because a boy at school beat her up. However, she quit because she was legally allowed to; by law she had to go to school until she was sixteen. By the time she reached that age, she had just failed her freshman year, and there was no way she was going to retake it. I left school in the same grade but, unlike Vickie, I wanted an education and, later on in my life, I started to study again.

Anna blamed her troubles engaging counsel in court on her bad communication skills and claimed that her illiteracy caused her to miscalculate things. In order to absolve herself, she testified in court that she had "trouble with zeros," saying: "[e]xamples are too numerous to chronicle but include writing '25.00' meaning $2,500 and '4500,00' meaning 4,500." She testified in court that she had "trouble with zeroes."

Her move to Mexia led to the now-familiar parts of the tale: the job at Jim's Krispy Fried Chicken; the marriage to Billy, a cook at the restaurant; the birth of her son Daniel when she was eighteen; and the divorce on the grounds of physical and mental abuse.

Shortly after claiming that the blonde haired, juvenile Billy Wade Smith was the love of her life, she filed for divorce. His simple-minded sensibility conflicted with her budding ambitions and he was always jealous of Vickie. He could not offer her what she wanted and their relationship ended in a messy divorce. She moved back to Houston when Daniel was under a year old, where she lived with Virgie for a few months. She tried to find work but the only jobs she could get didn't pay much: she worked as a cashier at Wal-Mart on Aldine Westfield, as a waitress at Red Lobster, and other going-nowhere places. For a while she was completely broke and had to go on welfare.

Billy was not paying any child support and she could not afford to raise her son on her own. She needed to focus on making a name for herself and so she dumped Daniel on her mother and moved into an apartment of her own.

CHAPTER 2

THE FLAT-CHESTED STRIPPER

"It's all make believe, isn't it?"

—MARILYN MONROE

Vickie's history as a stripper is part of the legend, but there's more to this than just the (forgive the choice of term) bare facts. A single mother desperate to make a better living, she chose stripping for the income she heard the girls were making.

She testified in court that, "One day on the way home from work, she passed a neon sign that displayed a lady in high heels wearing a bikini." This was her introduction to the world of strip bars. One club manager was willing to hire her, but only for the far less lucrative day shift. Even after giving birth, Vickie remained flat-chested, sporting what I call her "butchy" features. It was a liability to have her working in the club at peak hours.

Her first job in her new life was at a "gentlemen's club" called Rick's Plaza. Anna began to boast to friends that she would soon land a wealthy man. Completely self-serving and not the least bit embarrassed by it, she even bragged that her selfishness would make her rich and then she would come back and throw her success in the faces of friends and family.

Ritchie Avants, Rick's manager at the time she worked there, says that when she applied for the job as a stripper she was very innocent, though while in her teens, she had already bleached her hair blonde and she always had a very pretty face. She was hesitant about stripping and being photographed, but she would see it as an acting role and put on a persona to fit the part. At Rick's she changed her name to Robyn and played the role of a naïve girl.

One day, Anna's mother walked in to the strip joint. I think she may have been on duty. She caught Anna on the stage, got up there and dragged her off. However, there was not much she could do to stop her daughter from going back.

Anna was again hanging out with the wrong crowd, both at work and after hours. On a few occasions, one of her mother's co-workers had to go and get Vickie from a really nasty trailer park off Aldine Westfield. In the middle of the night, she was found higher than a kite, draped over a group of black guys.

Even though it was during the daytime, she drank heavily at work. One day she was performing on the runway and she was so drunk that she fell off the stage right onto a customer with a drink on his lap. Ritchie Avants says that he fired her on the spot, but it was not long before they rehired her again. He says that this process of hiring and firing Anna would repeat itself every three weeks.

The process of becoming a stripper is not as straight-forward as just getting up on the stage and stripping. It is a lot more sordid than that. Most strip clubs do not pay their girls to work there. Instead the strippers have to pay their manager for every night they dance in the club. The stripper makes her money in tips, lap dances and sometimes by getting a portion of the bar profits.

While a few girls are dancing, the rest are dotted around the club, either backstage or mingling with the customers. That is when the men get the opportunity to sleaze on the girls and try to convince them to go home with them. When this fails, the girls are offered money to perform sexual favors—at least a hand job, and sometimes sex in one of the private rooms or booths. Nearly all the girls eventually grant their customers sexual favors, and it is usually a prerequisite that they sleep with their manager also.

Anna wasn't happy at Rick's. She was still flat-chested, barely filling out an A-cup—not what men who frequent tittie bars come to see. The club manager was willing to let her work at Rick's during the daytime, but he would not give her the night shifts that she desired, as this is when the heavy spenders show up.

When she finally realized the manager wasn't going to change his mind, she quit. In 1991, after working on-and-off at Rick's for three years, Anna had a plan to overcome the problem that had blocked her from the better-earning night shift. The first step was to have her breasts enhanced. She paid for this with the money she had saved up from dancing and, naturally, with the financial help of her lovers.

What she designed for herself was such a leap in size that it had to be done in two stages. When finished, she had gone from an A-cup to a weighty, massive DD-cup, which eventually got increased to Double F's—obscenely large, but she was proud of them.

Dr. Gerald Johnson was known as the Breast King of Houston. He gave her what is called stacked implants. She got two 450 cc paddies, one that was placed above the muscle and the other beneath the muscle. This did not come without complications. Due to the extent of the increase in size, the extra weight of her breasts caused her all sorts of pain from back-, neck- and headaches to the pain of the added mass pulling at the tissue and pectoral glands, especially when she was not wearing any kind of support. Anna's family told me that she was in so much pain that she had to resort to medication. She took Xanax, Vicodin and other painkillers and she started drinking more heavily.

Soon after one surgery, the headlines were flashing, "Anna Nicole's boobs explode." This was almost true as one of her implants had leaked and she quickly had to get it replaced. Anna could no longer remember how many breast surgeries she had had. Not only had her implants leaked and been replaced on a number of occasions, she had also wildly fluctuated in size, making them bigger or smaller depending on her mood.

Driven by her determination to claw her way to a better life, Vickie modeled herself on her idol, another girl from poverty who had transformed herself into a sex goddess: Marilyn Monroe. She was obsessed with Monroe from the day she was born. She made sure posters of Marilyn were put up in every house she ever lived in and, as a teenager, she bleached her hair to look more like her. She always told her family she would grow up to be just like the legendary blonde bombshell and, right to the very end, she kept her promise.

The iconic actress was born Norma Jeane Mortenson in 1926 and as a child she was placed in a foster home. Her mother was diagnosed by doctors as being a paranoid schizophrenic and was institutionalized in the State Hospital in Norwalk, California. Like Anna, Norma Jeane was sent away, not to a relative but to the Los Angeles Orphans Home (later renamed Hollygrove), and then to a succession of foster homes where, it is said, she was sexually abused and neglected. The identity of her father remains ambiguous: various sources and biographies have been unable to agree on one man as being her biological father and even Marilyn's own claims conflict.

Just after Norma Jeane's first marriage, she was signed to the Blue Book model agency and that is when her transformation into a superstar began. She traded her long, brown, curly locks for a short, straightened golden-blonde hairstyle and, by twenty years of age, she had adopted the more commercially viable name that we all recognize…Marilyn Monroe.

And so, following in her role model's footsteps, Vickie metamorphosed into a radiant blonde with a curvaceous factory-made chest and a new name: Anna Nicole. She had previously used other pseudonyms such as Nikki and Robyn, but she chose Anna Nicole because she thought it sounded rich.

The physical transformations and a history of abuse are not their only common traits. Marilyn Monroe also posed naked and the shots ended up on the cover of the first issue of *Playboy*. Both blondes also had three husbands each, with both of their first marriages taking place before they were eighteen years old. At sixteen, Norma Jeane married an aircraft plant worker, Jim Dougherty. It was a marriage of convenience set up by her mother's best friend so that she could avoid going back to an orphanage. At seventeen—just after she had escaped from her mother's clutches—Vickie Lynn married a cook, Billy Smith, from whom she got her last name and son. Both of these marriages did not last very long.

Marilyn Monroe later married the American baseball hero, Joe DiMaggio (1954), and playwright Arthur Miller (1956-1961). More famously, she was also romantically linked to President John F. Kennedy, bringing with it trouble in a league of its own. Following suit, Anna Nicole Smith moved on to a billionaire Texas oil baron, J. Howard Marshall and, after he died, her attorney, Howard K. Stern.

Both of these women shared the same desperation for the limelight and both of them would do anything it took to get it. They were both very much dependent on men, using them to feel secure, financially and emotionally. Even after Marilyn Monroe became rich, she desperately needed a male shoulder to lean on.

Marilyn Monroe also had a history of drug addiction and an inclination to self-destruct. Marilyn never had children, but she desperately wanted them. She had a series of miscarriages, which toyed with both her mind and figure. During the filming of Billy

Wilder's *Some Like it Hot*, Marilyn Monroe's weight peaked to a size sixteen. Although no one remembers Marilyn for being overweight or fluctuating in size, she yoyo-ed back and forth as often as Anna Nicole.

Towards the end of her life, Marilyn was deeply unhappy. She failed to turn up to film sets and was hospitalized for depression several times during filming. When she did appear, she would involuntarily burst into tears, especially when in the presence of young children.

She was married to the writer, Arthur Miller, who wrote the movie *The Misfits* for her to star in. During filming, she had another miscarriage, which completely finished her off. Her marriage ended and she sank into deep depression. She lost a lot of weight and contradictorily looked as beautiful as ever. She was taking any kind of upper or downer she could get her hands on and started drinking heavily. She began filming her last ever role in *Something's Gotta Give*, and was fired and faced with a lawsuit thirty-two days into production. Two months later, on August 5, 1962, Marilyn committed suicide by allegedly overdosing on the sleeping pill, Nembutal.

Monroe was buried in a crypt at Corridor of Memories, #24, at the Westwood Village Memorial Park Cemetery in Los Angeles, California. Strangely enough, according to *Entertainment Tonight*, a friend of Anna's has been quoted as saying that "she always wanted to have a plot near [Marilyn Monroe's] and I believe one day that's where they'll probably both lie."

I'm not sure if life has imitated art because Anna fabricated a lot of her background in order to seem more like her idol. Her claims of abuse were hugely exaggerated—she may have been disciplined under a strict hand, but she was never badly hurt nor sexually abused. Anna always said that she came from a dirt-poor household, even though her mother had a stable job and income; and, despite what she said to the contrary, Anna did have a family, all of whom respected her for making a name for herself. We would have done anything to be a part of her life.

Another major difference between the two blondes is that Marilyn Monroe developed into a national star because of her acting career. She is remembered for her roles in cult movies that are still favorites half a century later. She was a conscientious actress and always looked for ways to improve herself. Monroe was concerned about the stereotypical ditzy blonde image branded on her and so the actress fled to New York, to study acting with Lee Strasberg (born Israel Strassberg). She married America's prestigious playwright, Arthur Miller, and worked with the most established actor of all time, Sir Lawrence Olivier. Despite her arduous attempts to be recognized as a talented actress and accepted by the big shots in Hollywood, she ended her life thinking she had failed.

Anna's most memorable acting role is in her recurring reality TV show. She will not be remembered for her acting ability and perhaps that is why she so desperately clung to the legend that preceded her. Marilyn Monroe was entirely original. She did not copy anyone because she didn't need to. Anna knew that she was not a talented actress, but she wanted to be a superstar anyway. She did everything to emulate her immortal idol, from undergoing cosmetic dental surgery to adopting her ditzy persona, which she thought looked cute on camera. Ironically, Marilyn Monroe played up the blonde stereotype that Anna Nicole epitomized.

Nothing could have interfered with Anna and her fame. It was her destiny. No matter how heavy, drugged up or untalented she was, there is no doubt the Texan had a larger-than-life personality. She was beautiful and, like her idol, the camera loved her regardless of how she felt inside.

Just as she had planned, Anna Nicole's physical changes brought her more income and the attention she had always craved from men. However, this attention was at the sacrifice of her son. She had never forgiven her mother for shipping her off to relatives as a teen, but now she continued to leave her son with his grand-mother so she could work as a stripper.

She fiercely focused on improving her lot in life, absolutely determined to succeed at whatever cost. For Anna, it was time to make money. She claimed that although she was interested in dancing, the idea of doing it nude made her stay away, at first. She initially started as a waitress, but it didn't take much convincing to get her to take off her clothes.

Now, I am not one to knock her because of the job, but the first question that springs to mind is why strip? I think for Anna this was the closest she could get to earning money for something she was good at. It's undeniable that she could attract attention, good or bad; this was her opportunity to get paid for having an audience.

Stripping is an industry that can become very lucrative if you work hard, put in long hours and build up a clientele that wants to come see you dance, get lap dances and personal attention. Is it the ideal way to earn a living? No, but many see it as the only way. As for Anna, it was her ticket to finding wealthy men, who would shower her with gifts and money for plastic surgery.

But I know that stripping is not the only way to get what you want. I worked at strip joints in Colorado and Michaels International in Houston, as a waitress and hostess for a few months. Throughout my life I used this employment as a way to make some quick cash, such as when I really needed the money after my divorce. I had to support three children on my own and this enabled me to do so.

Waitressing at the clubs, I was able to command a higher income than I ever had before, earning at least $2,000 a night. So I know you don't have to take your clothes off to make that kind of money. I was living at a level of comfort I hadn't known since I left home and, instead of getting drunk in order to get through a day of stripping, I got to know all the people that I worked with. I befriended the dancers and the customers and watched their interactions from a distance.

Many customers who came in would prefer to talk to the waitresses instead of the strippers because it felt less sleazy. The dancers were fine to look at and get lap dances from, but when it came to actually having a conversation, most of the men would rather talk to someone with their clothes on. They felt it was more of a challenge with us on the floor than the nude girls who were dancing. They paid me big tips and tried to offer me condos, vacations and cars. But I was there to earn money for my children and had no interest in the rest.

After she became famous, the clubs I worked at all knew I was Anna's sister and they expected me to be like her! I wasn't her, and I never once took my clothes off at these clubs.

You see, I know when to say when. I know when to walk away, or as Kenny Rogers says, "know when to hold them, know when to fold them, know when to walk away, know when to run."

Not my sister. Not Vickie Lynn Hogan.

Flaunting her new chest, Anna was hired at another Houston strip club, the Executive Suite on I-45 near Greenspoint Mall. They had billboards of her advertising the club. When it closed down to be turned into a landing strip, she moved on to Gigi's Cabaret. There is no shortage of strip clubs in Houston.

However, she did not immediately get upgraded to the night shift. Even after the transformation she had to prove herself by working the day shift first. She may have had huge boobs, but she still didn't have the look they were after. She was much bigger than the other models and her features made her look more masculine than the other waifs. It really got to her that they wouldn't give her the limelight that she felt she deserved and it made her even more determined to change her looks and rub it in everyone's face. She would tell us that she was going to make it big and then go back and shove it up their asses. She was always very determined to be rich and famous and she met just the right man to fulfill her desires.

In October 1991, during a visit to the club, a frequent patron spotted the new girl and was immediately drawn to her. This was no ordinary strip-joint customer, but J. Howard Marshall. A graduate of Yale Law School (one of the two or three most prestigious in the U.S.), he was brilliant enough to earn magna cum laude honors.

Though elderly and confined to a wheelchair, J. Howard Marshall was a regular customer at Gigi's. Due to his weak physical condition, he preferred to frequent the strip bar during the day, and that is how he met Vickie on her day shift.

J. Howard's wife and mistress had both died within a few months of each other and he was feeling particularly vulnerable. And who could have been better than Vickie at capturing his attention? With her newly enlarged boobs for him to grope, he fell under her spell.

He began pursuing Anna—asking her out, going frequently to see her. For several weeks she played hard to get, before agreeing to grant him special favors outside the club. He paid for hotel rooms, ordering room service for them, and took her to lunches at the River Oaks Country Club; he loved to walk into his hangout with a pretty woman on his arm. When she expressed concern that she was slacking off from her job, he compensated her with envelopes full of hundred-dollar bills.

She said she quit working the day after she met J. Howard. He was paying all of her bills and gave her $1,000-$5,000 in cash every time they saw each other. Why bother working if you don't have to? All her life she felt that someone else should pay her bills and here was the man to do just that.

She also always felt that she should not have to pay for any of the houses she lived in. She moved from her mother's house, almost immediately into the numerous homes Marshall bought for her. Even at the end of her life, she was living in her ex-boyfriend's million-dollar house in the Bahamas, under the pretext that he gave it to her as a gift.

The family all spoke of Anna's super-rich admirer as "Old Man Howard," figuring him for a pervert; they didn't believe a word of her protestations about how much she loved him and actually felt sorry for him. She probably even lied to herself for a minute, blinded by all that money flashing before her eyes.

Our brother, Donnie Hogan, once went for dinner at Red Lobster with J. Howard, Anna, Daniel, and her bodyguard. J Howard sat in his wheelchair and barely spoke. At the end of the meal he gave Anna a small wrapped box. When she untied the bow, Donnie saw more money than he had ever laid eyes on tied up in a bundle. Anna kissed J. Howard and said, "Oh thank you! You're so sweet!"

Anna's bodyguard was a bodybuilder. He was also her boyfriend, but J. Howard didn't know that. They had something going on for a long time, but kept it a secret. When Donnie went to stay with Anna in L.A., he witnessed the bodybuilder share her room. When Anna spoke to me, she barely mentioned J. Howard. She told me at length what he had given her and described every millimeter of her jewelry because she loved it so much. Anna told me a lot about the bodyguard she was having an affair with. She said she was completely heartbroken because he wouldn't leave his wife.

On their way to the restaurant, Donnie, Anna, Daniel and her bodyguard got stuck in slow traffic on the highway. They were driving in a new, big truck with bright lights. The people in the car in front thought Anna was flashing her headlights and they got really annoyed. The woman driving kept slamming the breaks to get the message across. In her soft voice, Anna was saying, "I'm sorry. I'm not doing anything. It's a new car." She flashed her lights at them to show she hadn't been before; they were just really bright. Obviously the people in the other car couldn't hear her and thought she was provoking them.

The woman stopped her car and her husband stepped out, trying to pick a fight. He stormed up towards them, looking all macho. Then Anna's bodyguard got out of the car to ask them what the problem was, but as soon as he appeared, the husband wimped out. He mumbled, "Not a problem man," and quickly got back in his car.

J. Howard installed Anna in a large house on a rambling fifteen-acre ranch, with horses in the barn that she rode often, various livestock and chickens, and enough servants to let her live like a queen. When J. Howard wasn't with her, he would call often, asking to speak to "the love of my life."

Anna lived alone on the Texas ranch that J. Howard Marshall had bought for her. It was out of the question that they live together, but she was often too scared to sleep in there by herself. Its enormity frightened her, even with all the doors locked. I guess she was afraid somebody might break in. She couldn't walk to the kitchen without worrying she might turn a corner and find a stranger.

Anna was always scared of being by herself. You could see this later on when she had her own show. Her son, Daniel, and attorney, Howard K. Stern, were filmed by her side twenty-four-seven. She used them as a security blanket and felt vulnerable the second they were not there.

Even the radio show KROQ questioned her about her bizarre situation with Howard K. Stern. It was along the lines of: Isn't it weird that Howard is your attorney and yet he does everything with you, including sharing a bed, while your dog is licking you, getting lap dances with you in Vegas, and generally never being absent from your side? She said, "So what? He's my best friend," and got annoyed that the interviewer had insinuated that their attorney/client relationship was not a conventional one.

While she was living on the ranch her answer to the problem was the same as the answer to so many of her other problems: make the Old Man buy her something—in this case, another house she could sleep in at night. The place she picked was in the nearby town of Spring, Texas. It wasn't much to look at, just a cute little brick house on an ordinary suburban street with a pick-up truck parked in every driveway and kids' bikes left out on the lawns. She didn't care; she hardly used the house except to sleep in.

She slept better when she had something warm to cuddle with. Sometimes if she was having trouble sleeping, she'd send her Aunt Elaine to the ranch to get one of the little lambs and bring it to her. She'd take it to bed and cuddle with it. Nothing kinky, it's just that Anna was an animal lover, and she could sleep better with that warm lamb to cuddle. Anna loved animals and she would share her bed with her pet sheep or pigs from the farm. She had a favorite lamb and when she was feeling lonely she would make Aunt Elaine go and get it for her to sleep with.

Even though Anna kept her distance from him, J. Howard Marshall became obsessed with her, constantly proposing and offering her more gifts every time she declined. He brought her rings that got bigger with each purchase. In April 1993, and the following Christmas Eve, J. Howard went to Neiman Marcus and, at Vickie's request, made the two most expensive purchases in the store's history, with each visit. There is only so much you can do with a $107,000 ring but to Vickie it was a game. Vickie later testified in court that J. Howard taught her to spend money, and that spending money was fun. As long as she was with him, there were no limits to the fun of spending money. He told her that to be somebody you had to look like somebody. Anna's years with J. Howard were like a child in a candy store where all the candy is free: she was allowed to have anything.

Meanwhile she was cheating on him at every turn, having sex with household servants, girlfriends, and married men. She has been romantically linked to body builder Clay Spires; actor Scott

Baio; John Travolta's nephew Rikki; radio personality Kristy Lee; real estate mogul Jonathan McManus; and even her own house-keeper. You would think that a lot of the stories that came out about Anna's sex life had been made up, but most of them were true. Anna loved sex, every way possible.

In Mexia, Anna had a long-term girlfriend, Sandi Powledge. Even though they dated for three years, Anna was very hesitant to speak openly about this relationship. Sandi had a tattoo of her former girlfriend displayed on her shoulder blade and whenever Anna saw it she would get jealous and insist that it be replaced with one of her. Eventually Sandi gave in and had Anna's face inked over her tattoo as a Christmas present to her lover.

Not all of Anna's lesbian affairs were kept as low profile. There was one report out of the United Kingdom that said Anna had a wild night of lesbian passion with a sexy barmaid.

The busty blonde, as they called her, had previously admitted to bisexual tendencies. This time she was playing bingo for charity at the Hollywood restaurant Hamburger Mary's when this attractive bar girl, said to be called Tracy, caught her eye.

According to reports, Anna immediately started flirting with the attractive blonde before heading home with her at the end of her shift. The next day, the barmaid came back to work boasting of her sexual escapades with Anna Nicole. She began showing off pictures of herself taken on her digital camera, handcuffed to a bed and covered in love bites.

A source is quoted in the *New York Post* as saying: "Tracy wasn't keeping it a secret. Anna Nicole put her in handcuffs and her neck was covered with hickeys."

"Anna Nicole was also doing that butt-slapping thing," the report said. "It was bizarre."

And then in 2004, *FHM* magazine wrote:

"Anna Nicole Smith claims she used to have sex with a ghost.

"The busty model (notice how everyone refers to her as the 'busty model,'—she just loved that) has revealed she had the supernatural sexual encounters several years ago—after mistakenly believing it was her boyfriend making love to her."

She revealed to *FHM* magazine:

"'A ghost would crawl up my leg and have sex with me at an apartment a long time ago in Texas. I used to think it was my boyfriend, and then one day I woke up and found it wasn't.'

"Anna Nicole admits she was scared at first, but soon realized she had nothing to fear because the 'ghost' was giving her 'amazing' sex.

"She said: 'I was freaked out about it, but then I was, like, Well, you know what? He's never hurt me and he just gave me some amazing sex, so I have no problem.'"

I think that story is ridiculous and, even with her reputation, I don't believe that there's any truth behind it. But hey, that's my sister. She'd say anything for publicity and when she didn't, they made it up anyway. All of these escapades kind of remind me of a Prince song, "Darling Nikki." That's the song where Prince sings "I knew a girl named Nikki, I guess you can say she was a sex fiend. I met her in a hotel lobby masturbating with a magazine…. She said how'd you like to waste some time and I could not resist when I saw little Nikki grind…."

Prince must have known Vickie in a previous life.

CHAPTER 3

PLAYBOY'S PLAYMATE
OF THE YEAR

*"I want to be the new Marilyn Monroe
and find my own Clark Gable."*

—ANNA NICOLE'S PLAYMATE
DATA SHEET 1992

*I*n 1992, Anna learned of a competition called the "Playboy Cover Contest." She had some naked pictures taken of her, sent them in, and landed on the magazine's March issue cover. They made her up to look like a refined debutante, dressed in an emerald-green, embroidered gown, and had her pose sitting in a dainty antique chair. The only evidence of her "big" personality is her blonde hair and smile.

Two months later she became "Playmate of the Month," and was featured in *Playboy's* centerfold. The naked pictures, biography, and "Playmate Data Sheet" were attributed to her married name, Vickie Smith. On the data sheet she wrote that it was her dream to become a playmate and that her ambition was to be "an actress, because I would like to be seen in the movies."

Her wish came true—at least partially. Just as Marilyn Monroe had been upgraded from "Sweetheart of the Month" to "Playmate of the Year" in 1953, exactly forty years later Anna

Nicole was named *Playboy's* "Playmate of the Year," annually chosen by Hugh Hefner. For this, she was awarded $100,000 and a Jaguar and she was put on the cover again in June 1993.

Just at it has done for other Playmates such as Jayne Mansfield (1955); fetish icon Bettie Page (1955); Shannon Tweed (1981); and Baywatch star Pamela Anderson (1990), the attention ignited Anna Nicole's career.

In 1992, the president of Guess?, Paul Marciano, quickly snapped her up and contracted her to replace Claudia Schiffer in their advertising campaign that year. Funnily enough, Guess? Jeans had started off their clothing label in the United States with a line of jeans that they named "Marilyn." Perhaps it was inevitable that Vickie would launch her career by modeling for them.

Apparently, Paul Marciano was the one who suggested her stage name, Anna Nicole, and since then she has not been called anything else. At first, he was not very impressed, but once her hair and make-up were done, she made love to the camera like no one else could. He immediately offered her a three-year, multi-million-dollar contract to represent Guess? on the condition that she could in no way harm the clothing line's flawless image. Anna just nodded and smiled.

Her voluptuous 5'11 hourglass (39-27-39) figure already resembled the features of a '50s starlet, so it was not too challenging to transform Anna Nicole into a Jayne Mansfield look-alike in the black-and-white photos. The camera fell in love with her immediately and, ironically, the most beautiful and sexy Anna ever looked was with most of her clothes on. Her photographer, Daniela Federici, was later quoted as saying, "Probably Anna was the sexiest thing I did."

It's funny how history repeats itself. Anna took the lead she was given and followed in the footsteps of the sex goddess she was emulating. The similarities between her and Jayne are even stronger than her resemblance to the more-classy Marilyn Monroe.

Jayne Mansfield's bust still remains a legend, measuring in at over forty inches. Anna, just one inch shy, shares the record of being the most well endowed *Playboy* cover girl in history. She soon discovered her enormous breasts could get her anywhere she pleased. Jayne had mastered this technique half a century earlier. From the age of fourteen onwards she refused to wear anything that restricted her breasts, including a bra. She let them prominently swing from side to side, like balloons flapping in the wind.

Jayne was famous for having her breasts on display. As if following in her footsteps, Anna Nicole would flash her boobs at every public event. In 1954, Jayne was invited to promote Howard Hughes' latest movie *Underwater*. She arrived in nothing but a pair of high-heels and a skimpy red bikini, struggling to hold itself together. In front of a barrage of press, she dove into the pool. Bursting through her bra, she left not one camera with spare film for the other actresses who hadn't yet arrived. Most importantly she captured Howard Hughes's eye, which would lead to the start of her lasting acting career. Anna made her splash when she dropped her top during the test shots for *Playboy*.

By the age of seventeen, Jayne was pregnant and, to her delight, this enhanced her boobs even more. (There are some claims that Anna's boobs got bigger because she was pregnant with Daniel, and while this may be true in part, there is proof that her famed proportions were obtained through surgery.) Jayne moved to Hollywood with her husband, pronouncing herself to Paramount Studios as their next new star. She kept her husband's name, Mansfield, because she felt it had "star quality"—sound familiar?—but she retained the Miss so as not to exclude any men from her fan base.

Jayne was involved in legal matters and was accused of abuse. After a series of car accidents—nine in as many months—she ultimately died in one. Two men both claimed to be Jayne Mansfield's husband and, in the same manner that Anna Nicole was to go to court over her late husband's ashes, these men fought over "their wife's" decapitated body. She did not have ashes to split though, and her corpse was buried under a heart-shaped grave in Los Angeles. Her funeral was a madhouse and almost the entire county's police force was needed to control the crowd.

One of Anna's co-stars has said that he didn't think anyone could ever be as kitsch as Jayne Mansfield, but Anna Nicole managed to live up to that role. Being presented as the spitting image of this '50s sex goddess enhanced Anna's career. Maybe it helped associate her public sex addiction with success. The photos also showed her to be a lot more classy than what was really behind the airbrushing and make-up—they made her look like a superstar.

Anna's second *Playboy* cover was a lot more conservative than the magazine is prone to. Perhaps this is because the same Guess? photographer, Daniela Federici, was responsible for the black-and-white *Playboy* photo of her. Anna posed with tousled, short, platinum-blonde hair, holding up a white garment that resembled the famous dress worn by Marilyn Monroe in the movie *The Seven Year Itch*. However, her uncanny likeness was again to the other sex goddess, Jayne Mansfield.

At first Anna modeled for Guess? in its San Antonio campaign and then went on to model for its Miami and New York campaigns. These photos were featured in top international magazines and on billboards across the world, giving Anna the tremendous exposure she desired.

In December 1993, she was featured in an advertising campaign for the Swedish clothing label, H&M, posing in cock-teasing underwear. I think this is a slight exaggeration, but according to imdb.com the provocative posters of her supposedly caused "several car accidents in major European cities."

In spring 1994, Vickie went to Singapore as the spokes-woman for Guess? Jeans. Allegedly, she was mobbed by fans and, feeling threatened by them, cancelled the remainder of the tour stops to Japan and the Philippines.

Shortly after she returned, she was bombarded with invitations to be a guest on all of America's evening talk shows, probably because they knew that she would guarantee them laughs at her expense, and the unscripted turmoil and shock factor that attracts viewers. She was interviewed on *E! Entertainment, Inside Edition, Entertainment Tonight, The Tonight Show, Larry King Live, Arsenio Hall, Regis and Kathy Lee, Howard Stern* (repeatedly), *Jimmy Kimmel Live*, and *A Current Affair*, which was later played in court during her probate trial over J. Howard Marshall's estate.

Around this time, Anna Nicole was desperate to be seen everywhere and be worshipped by the masses. On one of her visits to Aunt Kay, she begged her aunt and uncle and all of her cousins to get tattoos of her face imprinted onto their bodies. In order to convince them to actually get it done, she suggested that they do it as a birthday present to her. Her assistant, Kimmie, was another victim of Anna's self-promotional tactics. She too has had Anna Nicole's face immortalized on her arm. It is distinguished by her trademark bright-red lipstick, short-blonde locks and Marilyn Monroe likeness—the only thing that differentiates the two bombshells are Anna's disproportionately large fake boobs.

Later on, her reality show recorded Anna making Kimmie get another tattoo, this time of her autograph. Her friend, Frank, tells us that Anna had been asking him to get a tattoo of her for two years, until he finally relented and had her pin-up pose inked on his arm. He says it was intended to be a celebration of their lasting friendship. Her ex-lover, Larry Birkhead, got a cartoon sketch of Anna tattooed on his lower back "to show his devotion to her." However, the extent of Anna's self-obsession was perhaps made most clear by a tattoo of her own face she had imprinted on the calf of her leg.

Anna had a fetish with tattoos and felt that body art was the ultimate form of self-expression. Just before she died, she paid tribute to both of her children by getting tattoos of them on her shoulder blades. She had one of her together with her late son,

Daniel, which read "My Pumpkinhead," with the dates of his birth and death; and another of Anna with her baby daughter, Dannielynn.

Around the time of her Guess? campaign, Anna located her father and embraced him as her mentor and champion—the sex offender who had sexually abused me, her half-sister, and who she knew had raped her mother and her mother's sister. Even though Virgie had told Vickie it was the court that had made Donald stay away from his daughter, she insisted that it was her mother's fault they had been kept apart. Anna always had to rebel. If her family told her to stay away from her father, she had to go ahead and do the exact opposite. We saw Anna's betrayal as an attempt at retribution because her mother had sent her to live with relatives as a teenager.

Our dad never wanted me around Anna. I guess he was afraid that I would tell her the truth about what kind of a father he really was. We all thought Daddy was going to try to use her for all he could. I tried to tell Anna about the terrible things our father had done—the reason everyone had cut him off was because he was a bad person. He had molested me between the ages of five and nine, and he beat my baby brother black and blue when he was only two months old. Anna didn't want to hear any of it and she started screaming at me, "If you try to tell me anything bad about him, I'll never speak to you again." I was so upset, I cried for days.

The way Anna eventually found her father was through a private investigator. Once she had made a bit of money she wanted to celebrate her success with our father and so she hired a professional to track him down. Donnie was the one to pick up the phone when the investigator called. He passed over the phone to Donald, who was then asked if he would like to be contacted by his daughter. Donald, of course, jumped at the opportunity and said yes.

When Donald put down the phone, he told Donnie, "She must be rich. Sounds like she has a lot of money." He made this assumption because she could afford to hire someone to track him down. When Anna called, Donald turned on his "butt-kissing thing" and charmed her to the point of repulsion. He was only in it for the money.

Anna wanted to meet us and offered to fly us all out to California to stay with her. Donnie was scared of flying and chickened out, but Anna convinced him by promising an introduction to lots of celebrities and a trip to Disneyland. She had always wanted to go to the theme park. This was her chance to catch up on her childhood desires with her long-lost father and brother. Even though she had intended on taking me and Amy too, Donald told her that we were out of state and he couldn't reach us. For some weird reason he wanted it to be only the two men that got to accompany Anna in Los Angeles.

In fact, Amy and I were both living in Donald's house at the time and we had not gone anywhere. I found out that Donald had lied to Anna, but I didn't care. I was pregnant with my second child, Kayla, and I felt fat and unattractive. There was no way I was going to Hollywood looking like that! Amy was really livid. She was dying to go and was furious at Donald for lying. The next time I spoke to Anna, she worked out that Donald had lied to her and was really mad too, but it was too late to do anything about it.

Anna paid for Donald and Donnie's plane tickets and month-long stay at a hotel in Los Angeles. She picked them up in a limo and took them back to their hotel. She lived at the same hotel for most of the time in a separate room. She took them partying with her and, as promised, they met lots of celebrities.

Donnie found out from a hotel employee that his idol, Vince Neil from Mötley Crüe, was also staying at the hotel. They wouldn't give him Vince's room number though. Donnie went to Anna's room and told her that he was desperate to meet the musician and so Anna called down to reception and found out where he was staying. Anna called Vince and he immediately seized his opportunity to ask her out on a date. Even though she didn't particularly want to, she agreed to go for Donnie's sake. When they went out for dinner, Vince asked her to be in his music video, but she politely declined the offer. It wasn't her thing. She asked if he minded meeting our brother and he said that Donnie should go to his hotel room.

For some reason our dad insisted on accompanying Donnie. He doesn't even like Mötley Crüe's music, but he wanted to be in the limelight every step of the way. They hung out and he offered Donnie a beer. Even though Donnie doesn't drink beer, he accepted it. Donnie was dying to videotape them together and eventually plucked up the courage to ask Vince if he minded. Vince was very accommodating but said, "Not here, let's go downstairs." They went to the hotel garage and Vince showed Donnie his collection of cars. He had a Rolls Royce and selection of Ferraris; Donnie was speechless. Donnie filmed them together and our dad recorded his son with his idol, but later stole the film. Donald's a born thief and takes everything even if it means nothing to him. The only record Donnie has of their time together is a photo he had taken with Vince; he only managed to keep that by clinging to it for dear life.

Vince was living in the hotel at the time. He had recently split up with his wife and so he stayed at the hotel for about three or four months. Donnie hung out with him a few times and they went to a couple of clubs drinking together, but Anna stayed behind.

Donnie, Donald and Anna also went out to clubs together. Donnie wanted to go to a heavy metal club and Anna went to be a good sport, but she hated it and didn't stay long. Donnie and Donald would get really drunk and rowdy and Anna would chew them out the next day. She was very protective of them and wanted them to be happy and have the best time of their lives.

Anna took them to Disneyland with Daniel, her manager at the time, Melissa, and, of course, her bodyguard. Daniel and Donnie went together on all the daring rides. They spent a ton of money on the simulation ride, where you spin around upside down, and they loved the Michael Jackson 3D ride. Again they went by limo and taped themselves, as Anna was prone to do.

Anna took Donald and Donnie to the Playboy Mansion. They made silly home videos there. Donald would say things to the camera like, "I am one lucky daddy to be here, even if my daughter had to get naked to make it happen." He thought the world revolved around him and never tried to hide it.

Donnie was in utter bliss, mingling with the *Playboy* models. He talked to another Playmate, Barbara Moore, and could tell that his sister was envious. She said to Donnie, "Why are you talking to her?" even though to him the reason was pretty obvious. All the women in our family have a history of being jealous of other women. Whether they are friends, family or strangers, all women are competition.

You can now see Donald, Donnie and Anna in her Playmate of the Year video. It shows Anna provocatively saying she's daddy's little girl. On another clip at Anna's ranch she introduced Donald saying, "This is my dad. He's the light of my life." There are other bits on the video where she's doing sexy stuff, walking around her house naked, which she liked to do.

When they got back to Texas, Donald complained to his son, "It's tough when you want to do your own daughter." Donnie was repulsed, but barely surprised by our father's perversion, considering his reputation with women and young girls.

Anna spent a lot of time with her dad and Donnie, taking them to porn parties and social events. She took them to an MTV celebrity baseball event, which she was playing in. On the way there she kept singing the song, "If you think I'm sexy" over and over again to her father. She would always sing this song; everywhere she went she would sing, "If you want my body and you think I'm sexy come on sugar let me know." It was as if this was her warm-up song to motivate her into feeling sexy, not that she needed any help in that department.

She did strange things, like show Donald nude pictures of her in compromising positions. (She also tried to give me some of the photos, but I didn't want to look at them.) I don't care that Donald was not in her life for most of her childhood; a daughter does not give nude pictures of herself to her biological father and to a man who was a molester and pedophile. Anna knew his history of abuse, but she would still say provocative things to him, like "Don't my boobs look beautiful."

She was often exhausted when she finished working. She modeled all day and when she came back she would start stripping in front of Donnie and our dad and go straight to bed.

I thought about Daniel, Anna's son, and what it would mean for him to have this guy in his life. With Donald around Vickie and Daniel, I wondered if anyone was ever going to heal from the traumatic experiences our family had gone through.

However, our father could charm his way out of a paper bag and in Anna's eyes he could do no wrong. Donald would always be respectful towards her and she never got to see her father in his true light. Donnie and I spent time with her alone but there was always someone else around when she was with our father. He would go to events with her like the *Playboy* party, Disneyland, the MTV Awards and other functions, but they never spoke one-on-one.

Our father told Anna stories about his days in Vietnam. He had traded a chocolate bar and a pack of cigarettes for a spider monkey. He would joke about his pet monkey and how it pulled out his hair so Anna had to have a spider monkey too. She was advised that she should get a male monkey as female monkeys are competitive and violent, especially with other females. She ignored this and bought herself a girl monkey anyway. She had always wanted a daughter and I guess that is why she was more inclined to get a female pet. Just as she had been warned, the monkey would jump on her head and attack her. It would try to rip out her hair just as her father's pet had done to him. The monkey loved Anna's

Uncle Melvin, who lived with her at the time, but everyone else was scared of it and tried to keep out of its way. Then one day everyone went out, except Daniel. He fed it popcorn and accidentally killed the pet as it choked on the food.

After years of bringing up Daniel, Anna's mother called and said she wanted to go on a vacation with her husband and needed Anna to look after the boy. Living with his grandparents had been a happy, confidence-building time; Anna now took her son back with a vengeance, not just for the requested two weeks but permanently, as a vindictive way of punishing her mother.

She had sent him away for nearly all of the first six years of his life and then, once he had settled in to the new environment, she snatched him back because of an argument she had had with his grandparents. Anna had always wanted to eventually mother her son, but prioritized her career. The argument with his temporary guardian was her opportunity to take Daniel back.

Virgie admits that when she asked Daniel if he wanted to go live with his mother, he said that he did. She was after all his mother. J. Howard Marshall had bought Anna Nicole a house that they could live in and a nanny to look after her son so it was not like he would suddenly be accosted by the world of strip bars and sleaze. They definitely had financial support but, all the same, perhaps it would have worked out for the best if she had left him with his grandmother.

After I had my first daughter, Ashley, the doctors told me that they had found a tumor in one of my fallopian tubes and that I had to have it removed, along with one of my ovaries. I was seriously advised not to have any more children. A few years later I found out that I had somehow gotten pregnant and I was scared senseless. My doctor recommended that I stay in bed during most of my pregnancy and I was constantly upset that something would happen to either my child or me. On top of that I was not getting any child support from Ashley's father and I had no idea how I was going to look after my expanding family.

Our father knew how desperate Anna was for a daughter and, when he found out that I was pregnant with a girl, he tried to get her what she wanted. This was just after Anna had tracked Donald down and he would do anything to impress her. He knew she had money and thought that by giving her my baby she would have financially compensated him. My own father would have taken money from Anna in exchange for my children! That just shows how heartless and selfish he is.

She already knew that I had one girl and no husband and so when Donald informed her that my situation was desperate—that I was in poor health and pregnant with another girl—she jumped at the opportunity. Without his help, I don't think Anna would have approached me but, as joined forces, they tried to convince me that my children would be better off with her. Anna was very naïve and to her it probably seemed obvious. She had a big house and money, but she didn't have the daughter she wanted. I had one daughter and another on the way but I was nowhere nearly as well off as her.

I spoke to Anna a lot around that time. She was very flighty and difficult to pin down. She had a lot of jobs all over the world and practically lived in L.A. so I didn't get to spend that much time with her in Texas. It was much easier to chat with her over the phone. She hated talking about her past so we always discussed what she was up to with work and what her plans were. Even long-distance, we had a sisterly relationship. I have always been one to mother people and, although she was four years older than me, I would listen to her problems and try to give my advice. I didn't burden her with any of my dilemmas, but when Donald told her my situation, I was really hurt by her response.

Instead of offering me any support, she called me up and told me that I should give up my daughter, Ashley, and the child about to be born. She said that she would be more than happy to be their mother and "could give her a good life." Did she mean look after her until I got back on my feet? No way. She said, "I'll take her and she'll be my daughter. She'll be a little sister to Daniel."

There's more. "And when your new baby is born," she said, "I'll take that one, too." Like she was giving another "gift" on top of the first one. She desperately wanted a daughter. I knew that. Now she was trying to use my misery as a wedge to snatch my children away from me. I thought, "What kind of person could be so cold-hearted, especially to her own sister?"

I was living in Donald's house at the time, but I couldn't take the pressure. Deeply hurt, I decided to move to a different state to get as far away as possible; I could never imagine anyone else bringing up my children. Things were starting to look very promising for Vickie around this time. She was now a *Playboy* icon, international Guess? model, and she was about to have her own calendar published, but there was no way I could have given my children to her. She may have been successful at this point in her life, but who could guarantee that her career would last? I know how the industry works, you reach your peak and then it can go in any direction. How could I be sure she wouldn't end up as a junkie in Hollywood bringing Daniel and my children down with her?

On top of that, her celebrity status was not the kind that I would want my children to be associated with. Her fame erupted around the time she was having an affair with a man sixty-three years older than her, not the kind of relationship I would want my daughters to aspire to be in when they reach twenty-six.

I was so shocked by Vickie's response that I had to get away. I moved to Wyoming with my other half-sister, Amy. Her husband lived there and she told me I should move close to her. Once I got to Wyoming, I got a job at a dry cleaners and went back to school. I stayed at a homeless shelter until I had saved up enough money to rent a place of my own and, within a month, I moved into a two-bedroom apartment.

Up until the end of my pregnancy, Anna was hoping I would change my mind and give up my babies. She told me I had to call her when I was going to the hospital to deliver and her reason wasn't hard to figure out. She wanted to catch me when I was too tired to argue and get me to say she could take Ashley and the new baby.

I called her when I was about to go to the hospital. At the last moment, I wanted to have my sister at the hospital with me and show her that I would be a good mother.

When I called, Aunt Elaine answered the phone and said, "She can't come, Donna. She's off shooting a movie called *Naked Gun 33 1/3*, and she can't leave the set today." And Aunt Elaine said, "She'll be real disappointed." I think Anna must have forgotten by then. The idea of mothering my daughters was just a fleeting obsession, encouraged by our father. I am so happy I stood firm and struggled to keep my girls. I have since had a son, and I am proud of all three of my children: Ashley Elizabeth, Kayla Victoria, and Brandon Armandos.

CHAPTER 4

CALENDAR SIGNING

"Probably Anna was the sexiest thing I did."

—DANIELA FEDERICI

*I*n 1994, Anna was fussed over by a crew of hair stylists, manicurists and makeup artists. Then she stripped and stepped in front of the cameras. This was the first day of photography for the now infamous Anna Nicole pinup calendar, released by the Landmark calendar company. Taking her clothes off in front of a crowd was no challenge for her, of course. After all those years working the gentlemen's clubs, naked was, for Anna, just a way to earn money.

Behind the still camera that day was one of the hottest photographers in the States: Daniela Federici, an Australian-born Italian. She was snapped-up straight from film school by Paul Marciano. Her first major photography job was the Guess? campaign with Anna Nicole and, she never stopped working with scads of big-name celebrities. She did shoots with movie stars like Isabella Rossellini, Sharon Stone and Catherine Zeta-Jones; models like the breathtaking Heidi Klum and Cindy Crawford; musicians Debbie Harry and Prince; and even sports stars, Venus Williams and David Beckham, along with his wife, Victoria.

From the time of her very first *Playboy* photo shoot, Anna said she thought it was really tacky to expose her nipples and was very particular about what she would and wouldn't show. There are obviously a few exceptions, like her test shots for *Playboy*, and later when the temptation of money and increasing fame would be too much for her to resist. That's not to say that Anna refused to pose nude, but she made sure that at least her hands were concealing her private bits. With Daniela calling the shots, Anna got into a series of sexy poses. Anna left the most personal parts of her anatomy to the imagination and made a big deal of the chest she was so proud of.

A few months later, in November, the calendar was being put on sale with much fanfare. An entire PR team had been at work for weeks trying to stir up interest. After all, Anna had already been the Guess? Jeans spokesperson, *Playboy's* Playmate of the Year and, when she married the Old Man, she had landed enough publicity to make the most famous international movie stars envious. My sister loved the spotlight; she *needed* it.

Anna called me one day in November. The calendar was going on sale the next day, and she was scheduled to do a signing at one of the biggest bookstores in Houston. Like some young writer trying to build sales for her first novel, she was panicked that she would sit at a little table at the bookstore and people would walk past and not even notice. Or even worse, feel sorry for her. It must be terribly embarrassing to sit at a table with your pen ready and no one paying any attention. Anna would have had a meltdown.

Making sure that there was no way this would happen, she went around calling friends and family in the area and insisted that they had to come to her signing. You don't say "No" to Anna Nicole; she doesn't understand the word. But when she called me, it didn't take much convincing; I actually wanted to go. I'm proud of my sister. Even if she hadn't been nice to me, she started from nothing and made herself into a big celebrity. I think that's something to be proud of and I don't care what anyone says about how she did it. She got her start in that little Texas hick town of

Mexia where there's not much else but dust, a gas station, two eateries, and more dust. She came from a broken family, with an abusive father, and she married a man who beat her. If you had all that in your life do you think you could be famous today?

I had that same background, and all I had to show for it was two kids who didn't have a father, stuck in the same rut I'd always been in. No wonder I thought my sister was doing something right.

So I took my daughters, Kayla and Ashley; my new husband (I'll call him Mike); and my grandma, Memal, to the calendar signing. It was coming up to Anna's birthday and so I bought her a collectible Marilyn Monroe doll from Toys "R" Us as a gift.

When we showed up at the bookstore the next day, we couldn't find any place to park. I thought there must be some street fair going on, or maybe a festival, because there were cars stashed everywhere, even on the median strip. When we finally found a place to leave my disastrous truck, we discovered what the fuss was about. There wasn't a street fair; it was Anna's signing that had brought all these people out.

The bookstore was packed with more folks than had probably ever been in the place since it opened. Paparazzi were shooting off their flashbulbs. Two local TV stations were taping for their evening news shows.

People were buying the calendar and then trying to get in line to have Anna sign it. But the line was so long that the end of it got lost in the crush of people packed in shoulder to shoulder. Up front, Anna looked like a million bucks in a long sparkly gown and her million-dollar necklace. I had never seen a more beautiful woman in my life.

I knew Anna was expecting us to join her at the table where she was sitting. We wanted to work our way toward her but every time we tried, people glared, elbowed us, and shoved us to the side of the store. These folks were really *rude*. Some of her fans were so mesmerized by Anna, it was like watching children in line for the latest PlayStation.

I also overheard remarks being made by people in the crowd, who were condemning her. "She's just so fake." "She only got famous by being naked most of her life." "She's just another dumb blonde." These were people who had come from who-knows-where to see Anna Nicole up close. They had bought their calendars and they were waiting, maybe for hours, to work their way to the table and have her autograph them, but now they had nothing better to do than trash my sister. A lot of spiteful people said she was not worth waiting in line to see, so they just hung around on the sidelines. I couldn't work out why they would bother to come all this way only to bitch about Anna while she was in the room.

One woman said something nastier than all get-out and I lost it. I heard her cutting Anna down, talking about all the surgeries that it had taken her to look like that. "She only looks a million bucks because it took her that much money to get there."

It's one thing to trash someone you are close to but it's quite another to hear a stranger dissing your family. Anna and I may have said bad things about each other, but we would be damned if someone else said anything mean about either of us.

I'm not exactly a genteel angel to begin with and I was really nervous in front of all these people. I automatically went to my sister's defense and shouted, "Bitch, if you don't like her, just get out of here." The lady looked at me like she was about to fix her hands on my throat and start choking me if her husband didn't do it first. Just then Anna spotted me in the crowd. She called my name, waved, and pointed me out to two policemen standing guard at her table. They came pushing through the crowd to get us and escorted us back to join her.

At that moment, I was so proud of Anna. Standing next to my gorgeous sister made me feel special. All these people had gone to great lengths to see Anna and, when each of them finally reached the front of the line and handed her their poster to sign, they only had nice words to say. "Oh, you're so beautiful," they said to her. "Oh, can I hug you?" "Can I have a photo with you?"

Anna Nicole stayed two extra hours until she had signed a calendar for everybody who wanted her autograph. She wanted to fly high and be adored. She fed off their adoration. I had just heard firsthand how cruel those people can be at a distance, but up close, it seemed to Anna, they were completely infatuated with her.

I stood behind the star with Daniel, Aunt Elaine, and Anna's best friend from childhood, Debbie. Debbie had become the owner of a beauty shop, and she served Anna as a personal assistant, doing her hair, nails and makeup.

I was holding Kayla up there with me. I was wearing a frumpy sweater and felt like the ugly sister. I was scared people would compare us, especially with all of those judgmental people looking straight at me. I made certain Kayla was in my arms to divert as much attention away from me as possible. Of course, Anna constantly played with the baby; it made her look good. She didn't pay much notice to the rest of us though, as she was too busy being admired. But who could blame her? The night before, she was so worried no one was going to come to see her that, when they did, she reveled in their adoration. Once she got a taste of all those people idolizing her, she would never be the same again.

When the signing was due to finish, we all went back to what we called "The Spring House." Anna stayed behind because she didn't want to let any of her fans down. She was scheduled to catch a flight that evening and so I didn't think I would see her again. I was quite relieved because, although I wanted to spend some time with her, I didn't want Anna to formally meet my husband. I knew that she wouldn't approve and I didn't want her to look down on me.

Aunt Elaine was looking after Daniel, so Debbie, my family and I went back to the Spring House with them. We were just hanging out and there were other people who were part of Anna's entourage that I didn't know. Then Anna surprised us all by showing up with her chauffeur and the rest of her entourage. I thought she was going to go right to the airport so it was a real shock to see her walk through the door. It turned out that she wanted to say goodbye to all of us and pack some things to take with her.

She stayed for a few hours and we watched the TV news shows to see the stories about the event; of course they had things to say that weren't kind. Aunt Elaine and I were upset, but Anna just said, "Bad publicity is good publicity," which meant she didn't particularly care what they said as long as they were focusing on her. "As long as they're talking about me, I'm alive," she explained.

She had been trying to get me to come to California with her, promising that she would find me a rich husband to marry. I'm a small-town Texas girl, born and bred. I look like I'm small-town Texas, I talk like I'm small-town Texas, and I act like I'm small-town Texas. Put me in a room with a bunch of rich Los Angeles guys and I wouldn't know what to say to them. I'd be so sure of saying something that would make them all turn around and walk away, I just couldn't see my sister showing me off to some big-deal businessman, movie producer or studio executive.

I ruined Anna's grand plans to find me some rich man who would marry me and take care of all my wants. Instead, I'd gone and married a Hispanic guy—a local with no money and little hope of ever having any. I'm not like Anna, I don't like to put on a show and I don't have her overwhelming drive for money and success.

Maybe marrying a man with no money and nothing going for him wasn't the best plan either, but at the time I thought it was a good idea. I married Mike because I felt pressured. I had two little girls without fathers and Mike had been a friend for some time. He was good with my daughters, comfortable to have around, and he didn't have any of the bad habits of alcohol or drugs like so many of the other men around Anna and me. I thought that with Mike I could settle down and we'd be like a real family.

Anna had been trying to talk me out of marrying Mike and, when Aunt Elaine introduced them, she did nothing to hide her disapproval. Mike was sitting on the edge of the couch and Anna was standing in front of him when Aunt Elaine said to her, "This is your new brother-in-law." Mike stood up to shake her hand, but she refused to reciprocate. Instead she looked at him and said, "Great—all I need is a new brother-in-law," then turned and walked away.

It was like she had spat in his face. He tried to pass it off as nothing, but I could tell he was really hurt. Anyone would be. But what could I have said? Naturally, no matter what I tried to tell Mike, he thought it was because he's Hispanic. No, Mike, it was because you were as poor as me and without any kind of promising future.

Maybe I should have listened to Anna on this one. Mike and I separated after two years and we divorced. I guess I never loved him enough and I thought it wasn't fair to him. I only regret that when he left, he kept a lot of my family pictures, probably hoping to sell the ones of Anna and pocket the money. Maybe she was right about him after all.

That whole day, Anna was trying to play with my girls. It was obvious she was desperate to have a daughter of her own and by making a fuss over my one-year-old Kay Kay, Kayla's nickname, she also placed herself in the limelight. At the signing she ignored Ashley, the elder of the two, and carried Kayla as if she was a trophy. Kayla didn't like it though. She was a very shy child and would always cling to me and hide from strangers. Anna kept wanting to hug her or touch her but, every time she did, Kayla started to scream and cry. Anna was completely baffled by this, saying, "Why don't you love me? All babies love me."

When we got to the Spring House, Anna managed to win over Kay Kay. At the time her favorite snack was bread and butter pickles. She always had a huge jar of them at the house and she would spread the pickles across her plate and sprinkle salt on top. She popped one into Kay Kay's mouth and my daughter loved them. She kept running back for more until she and Anna had eaten them all. Kay Kay started crying, she was so upset that there were no more left. Anna tried to placate her by giving her a dill pickle, but she only liked the bread and butter kind. It's funny because ever since then, I have been completely hooked on them too. I always get cravings for bread and butter pickles with extra salt sprinkled on them and it reminds me of that day with Anna.

Soon after, Anna and I were off in a room away from the others. She had done a commercial for Conair hair products that I wanted to see. I picked up a videotape sitting by the television set and she said, "Oh, no, Donna—don't look at that one right now. You can see it later if you want to, but I don't want anybody else in the house to see it." She hinted that it was Debbie and her in a porno, but I have no idea if that was true. Maybe I assumed it was Debbie because she was in the house at the time. It could just as easily have been one of her lesbian ex-girlfriends that I didn't know.

She said that I could have the tape if I wanted. I thought it was pretty weird that Anna would even dream I'd have any interest in watching a video of her having lesbian sex. I haven't seen all that many adult videos but the idea that anybody would want to watch her own *sister* having sex? I told her, "No, never mind."

Anna showed me a picture of the actor Tim Robbins that she had taped to her wall and started kissing it. She told me, "I just love him, he's my sweetheart." She thought he was God's gift to earth. She told me she had had an affair with him while they were shooting *The Hudsucker Proxy* together. Susan Sarandon was either heavily pregnant or had just given birth to her son at the time and Anna said that if he wasn't married to Susan she would be with him.

Anna had a stack of fan mail that she pulled out. She sorted through it and we had a laugh over some of the letters. The things people sent her were really freaky. They sent in nude pictures of themselves and she showed me one of the girls who had written to her. She had sent in a completely naked photo of herself and had written to Anna that she was in love with her and thought that they should be girlfriends. It was scary, to the point of stalking, and then Anna laughed and told me this girl was one of her more persistent fans.

Anna gave me photos of herself to keep, some of which were of her posing nude. I didn't know what to say because I really didn't want any nude photos of my sister. All I needed was to have sexy, explicit photos of Anna in all her glory, lying around the house for my husband to find. She autographed a few for me and wrote short notes on them. On one of the pictures she wrote around the photo: "Follow your dreams, make them come true. Love your big sis. Vickie Lynn a.k.a. "Anna Nicole.""

Vickie had adopted a persona and always put up a front. She was no longer the same person she had been, even in front of me. Sometimes she let her guard down, but she was so consumed with being Anna Nicole that it was very difficult to tell who she really was. She wanted everyone else to be obsessed with her. That is why she made all her friends and family get tattoos of her face and name, and why she always gave everybody autographed photos of herself. She was in love with the idea that everybody had a piece of the new her.

While Anna and I were sitting together, a realtor friend of hers came in. Anna was thinking of selling The Spring House and buying something else. In fact, she had been trying to talk me into taking the house off her hands. Like I could just walk into a bank and they would give me a mortgage. With my credit history, I'm not exactly the kind of person that banks are in a big rush to lend money to. I could just see myself filling out an application and listing the homeless shelter as one of my previous addresses and "welfare" as a one-time source of income. With all the money the Old Man had been laying on Anna, she had never once lifted a finger to help me. But now she wanted me to buy this $300,000 house from her. That was a laugh.

Her realtor came in and almost the first thing he said was, "Where's the coke?" Anna got a little flustered. She said, "Shhh—not in front of my sister." Only she said it loud enough for me to hear. Just because I was in school for Criminal Justice at the time, did she think I was going to go to the cops and turn her in?

She tried to cover up by telling the realtor, "The Coke's in the refrigerator, of course, where it always is." That was supposed to fool me, so I'd think he was talking about soda, not something to snort. It was a private joke between them; I doubt the realtor would have asked for drugs so indiscreetly.

Anna tried to be really generous and told me that I could borrow any of her clothes that I wanted. She insisted that I go through her wardrobe and pick something out, but there was no way I would wear her clothes. For a start I wouldn't even be able to fit in them.

I pulled out this slinky top and Anna told me I should try it on because it's stretchy. She told me not to worry about my weight as her figure fluctuated all the time. I know from pictures that she had yoyo-ed from about 140 lbs. in 1992, to 224 lbs. in 1996, 138 lbs. in 1997, back to more than 200 lbs. in 2002, during her reality show, and then back down in 2005 to her early 1990s weight. She said that was why she tried to only buy stretchy clothes. I also noticed that her thousands of dollars worth of dresses ranged from size 8-14 so that she always had something to wear no matter how much weight she had gained or lost.

I gave Anna the Marilyn Monroe doll that I had bought for her and she loved it. I told her where it was from and she was like, "Oh I love Toys 'R' Us!" and since then she has bought the whole collection. She was so obsessed with Marilyn Monroe, she wanted to have everything related to her.

I've always loved her blonde, adorable son Daniel. He was nine at the time of the calendar signing and annoyed because he thought he looked kind of girlish with his hair as long as it was, but his mother wouldn't let him have a haircut. I always found Daniel to be a real sweetie, which I think is a huge mystery with Anna for a mother; considering all the awfully strange ways she treated her own child.

He must have had a tough time getting used to living with his grandparents and growing attached to them and then being taken back again by Anna. Once I heard a preacher say that the reason grandparents and grandchildren get on so well together is because they have an enemy in common. So maybe that explains why Anna's mother, Virgie, was a parent who hated us, and who both of us came to hate while we were being raised, but then turned out to be a gift of a grandmother to Daniel. Maybe it was his time with his grandmother that turned him into such a nice kid despite having Anna as his mother.

Anna constantly embarrassed her son in public but the night of the calendar signing she really excelled herself. She started saying, "My boobs still have milk in them even though I haven't had a child since Daniel, and that was nine years ago." Daniel was already squirming, but she kept right on. She said, "I could still breast feed him," and she grabbed him by the back of the neck, pulled his head down to her chest, and rubbed his face deep into her boobs. Daniel is such a sweetheart that he didn't even blow up at her over it. He just said, "Mom, I hate it when you do that," and walked away.

Two weeks after the calendar signing I found out that I was pregnant with Brandon. I told Anna immediately but she thought I had kept it from her at the signing, especially when I gave birth eight months later. She must have thought that because she had wanted my girls so desperately before, I didn't want to tell her I was having another baby. However, that's not true. Until about a month after Brandon was conceived, I had absolutely no idea I was pregnant with him.

A few months later, I went to see Anna at her house. My children loved it at the ranch because they could play on the swings. Anna had a motorcycle and I was shocked that she knew how to drive it. I couldn't even get the kickstand up; the Harley was so heavy. She would practice riding up and down her long concrete driveway and Daniel would tail behind her on his little dirt bike. It was so cute.

Even when Anna was away, Aunt Elaine and Daniel stayed at the ranch. I sometimes went to visit and let the kids play on the swings. It was about an hour away from where we lived and they loved it there. I wish I had made more of an effort to see Daniel before it was too late.

CHAPTER 5

THE LOST SISTER

"Where's Melissa Lynn Hogan?"

—DONNA HOGAN

Ever since I was born, I have known that somewhere out there we have another sister. Melissa Lynn was born in Texas in 1976. She has the same father as Anna, Amy and me, but her mother is allegedly a woman named Ann. Since Ann was unfit to care for her, Melissa was given to a family to raise, and later adopted. We never saw her again.

I have asked my parents time and time again where Melissa could be and how I can find her, but they are equally incapable of delivering any answers. My father never told me anything because he doesn't want Melissa to be found. As far as he is concerned, Melissa is just another daughter who will come back to haunt him. He already feels guilty about being such a bad father to Vickie, Amy and me, the last thing he needs is to have a fourth daughter to add to his conscience. He is also scared that, if she turned up, Melissa Lynn might claim years of unpaid child support.

Until Anna hired a private detective to find him, Donald would never have known about her whereabouts either and he wouldn't have cared. The only reason he was at all interested in Anna was because he could sense she had money.

All I know is that Donald told me that Melissa is the daughter of Ann, a woman he was dating just after my mother. When I asked him for her last name so that I could try to track her down, he told me it was Aldberry. When I asked him again, he told me that it was Aldmann, but there are lots of variations of the spelling and he refused to clarify which it is. Then one day he had enough of me pestering him for answers about my sister and he blurted out, "Why don't you ask your mother? She gave birth to her."

I couldn't believe what he had just said and I'm still not sure if it's true. I have persistently asked my mother who Melissa is. I know that, up until Melissa was a few months old, she lived with us on and off. My father was living with his girlfriend, Ann, and my mother, Wanda, was looking after me, and her other two kids. Sometimes we visited our dad and occasionally Melissa came to stay with us at our Mom's house. Wanda always called Melissa, Missy Lynn, as a baby, and so the name has stuck.

Due to my mother's unfortunate mental state, I have never been able to get straight answers from her. The only thing I have been able to work out is that the facts don't add up. My grandmother on Donald's side has always said that she doesn't think Ann gave birth because she never looked pregnant. What is more is that right after Amy was born, my mother did one of her disappearing acts for almost a year. During that time no one could track her down. My mother also swears that nine months after Amy was born, she had an abortion with Donald's child. This is exactly around the time that Ann supposedly gave birth to Melissa.

All this information I have pieced together is too much of a coincidence to ignore. I tried asking my mother for more information but she would go through crazy spells, during which nothing she said made any sense. At times she would enter a deep depression and nothing could snap her out of it. She would rock on the floor crying for hours on end and, on more than one occasion, I have heard her sob, "I wish I'd never given her back to them." I can only assume that she was referring to Melissa. Why would she cry ceaselessly unless she was referring to her own daughter? Perhaps I am being too presumptuous, but I can't think of any other explanation.

It also makes me think that perhaps it was the agonizing ordeal of giving away her daughter that has made her so mentally unstable. They say that traumatic experiences can trigger mental illness and I cannot help but think that giving up her baby, Melissa, contributed to Wanda's insanity.

I have tried desperately to find my missing sister, but so far I have been unsuccessful. I can't comprehend why Vickie had no desire to find her; she never wanted to even talk about it. She was too preoccupied with her own budding success to care. I have always wanted to find Melissa because I thought it would complete the family and somehow might help my mother get better.

There are so many things I'd like to say to her and so many things I'd like to hear from her. Maybe she can fill in all the missing pieces to the puzzle that my father has adamantly refused to provide. It is still very unsettling to me that I don't know where Melissa Lynn is, or even if she is my mother's daughter.

I thought that, with Vickie's fame, we'd be able to find her or she would find us. She must have seen Vickie on television, in a magazine or on the news and I thought that would make her reach out. Perhaps it's what Vickie had become that has turned our sister away and dissuaded her from reaching out. Maybe she simply doesn't want to get involved in this media circus and who could blame her? I did manage to do some investigatory work without Anna's help and found someone living in Colorado called Melissa Lynn Valentine. I also found out that her maiden name is Hogan and I tried to contact her, but without success.

All I know is that there are a lot of unanswered questions and it is very weird that I am the only one who seems to have noticed. At one point, my sister Amy also tried to find Melissa but our father threatened her and made her stop. I can't work out why Melissa's whereabouts is such a big secret. Losing Anna has only strengthened my commitment to find our lost sister.

CHAPTER 6

J. HOWARD MARSHALL II

> *"Men in love do stupid things
> and I was sure guilty"*
> —J. HOWARD MARSHALL II

J. Howard Marshall II was born on January 24, 1905 in Germantown, PA, and, by all accounts, he led an extraordinary life for more than nine decades. His career spanned almost the entire history of the oil industry, from the early years when uncontrolled production depleted valuable fields and natural gas was burned at the wellhead, to the decades of energy shortages and the Arab oil embargo.

According to the research done on him for Vickie's bankruptcy court case in California, he was one of the few "self-made entrepreneurs who shaped our country." He is described as an "enterprising pioneer" and one of the individuals from the turn of the last century whose character and vision survive in both mythic and real legacies. His life story is so bizarre that by the end you cannot help but expect Anna Nicole Smith to play a role in it. I am excerpting from his background, researched and summarized by Judge Carter for the California District Court, so that you can truly fathom the real events of his life.

"Born in 1905, J. Howard attended private schools in the northeast part of the United States, including the George School, an exclusive New England prep school, Haverford College, an elite liberal arts college, and Yale Law School, one of the nation's leading law schools, from which he graduated magna cum laude in 1931. Although he often derided his undergraduate liberal arts education, he took great pride in the legal training he received at Yale. Upon graduation, he worked as an associate in a New York firm for two years. Subsequently one of the subjects he taught at Yale was wills and trusts. Surely he did not realize at the time that these same subjects would take up large portions of his later life, and dominate his family's affairs for more than six years after his death."

After various high-powered positions in the petroleum industry, in 1954, J. Howard was one of the founders of Great Northern Oil and Gas Company (now Marathon Ashland), where most of his wealth stems from. With sales and operating revenues of $9.3 billion in fiscal 2005, Ashland ranks among the nation's top 500 companies based on revenues. Great Nothern Oil and Gas Company was also developed into Koch Industries, estimated to be the second largest privately run company in the United States, based on revenues of approximately $35 billion. J. Howard eventually formed Marshall Petroleum in 1984 and also became a successful independent oilman.

J. Howard married his first wife, Eleanor M. Pierce, in 1931. "[She] has been described to the Court as a refined, gentile [sic], spiritual, and religious woman." They had two children together: J. Howard Marshall III and E. Pierce. The children were mainly brought up by their mother. Their father was always away working and they never got to spend much time with him.

J. Howard Marshall III is the elder son. He is the one who was accused of conspiring with Anna Nicole against Pierce in order to get some of his father's money. In 1974, J. Howard Marshall II gave both of his sons some of the voting common stock of Koch. However, the elder son was apparently too clever for his own good.

He went against his father's wishes and voted for the company to go public. The father was then forced to pay $8 million to buy the stock back from his own family—a lot more than it was worth—and so he disinherited the elder son. He considered the $8 million to be an advance. I bet J. Howard Marshall III regrets that sneaky move now!

In order to make sure something like that never happened again, J. Howard changed the estate plan. He made sure that his eldest son was completely excluded from the inheritance. The will in 1982 stated that only Bettye (his wife at the time), and upon her death, his youngest son Pierce were his sole heirs.

Pierce was married in 1965 and he and his wife were married for over thirty-five years. Since his recent unexpected death, Pierce's spouse, Elaine Tettemer Marshall, has vowed to fight for every last cent on her late husband's behalf.

Pierce worked in California and New York as an investment banker. In 1968, his father wanted him to move to Texas so that he could learn about his oil and gas ventures and later take them over.

As Pierce had never previously gotten to know his father, this move gave them the chance to bond and they built up a strong father-son relationship. Throughout the remainder of the 1960s and 1970s, Pierce and J. Howard invested together in businesses which ranged from oil and gas to restaurant ownership.

"In 1961, after being married for thirty years, Eleanor and J. Howard divorced and two trusts were created to hold J. Howard's and Eleanor's now separate property interests…. However, Eleanor left her financial affairs in the hands of her former husband because she trusted his business acumen.

"In December 1961, J. Howard married Bettye Bohannon. At his father's request, Pierce served as the best man. There are no children from this marriage. Bettye and J. Howard had met in the mid-1930s. She has been described to the Court as strong, intelligent, street smart, astute in business, and a good match for

J. Howard. J. Howard Marshall III always believed that his father had a long-term relationship with Bettye during his marriage to Eleanor.

"In 1961, J. Howard accepted the Presidency of Union Texas and he and Bettye moved to Houston. When most people are planning for retirement, J. Howard was continuing the pursuit of the business that had been the focus of his life. J. Howard created what he referred to as a 'new community' for himself and Bettye. Although not formalized until years later, to J. Howard this new community always existed. It consisted of any assets that he and Bettye acquired during their marriage, even if they could be traced back to his own separate property."

Similarly, J. Howard later promised Anna half of his "new community," the assets that were acquired during his marriage to her.

"In the early 1980's Bettye was diagnosed with Alzheimer's disease. Her condition slowly deteriorated until her death in the fall of 1991...making J. Howard the only heir to his estate.

"In 1982, J. Howard met 'Lady' Diane Walker. Feeling the need for a drink after a day at the office, he went to a 'strip joint, a tittie bar' as he described it in his videotaped deposition in 1992. Lady Walker was one of the strippers who took everything off for J. Howard in return for his generous dollar bills. Thus, at the age of seventy-eight, he began his pursuit of Lady Walker.

"J. Howard wanted Lady Walker to be his exclusive mistress and he often professed his desire and commitment to marry her if Bettye died." He gave her tons of money and gifts and cryptic love letters always promising her more.

"These letters contain repetitive and aggressive protestations of his love, always coupled with a reference to money.

Dear Lady
I fear I am a nuisance—I still hope I am a beloved nuisance—
of course
I shall do what you ask 'stop calling'…it is part
of the juice of my devotion… All of this is a far, far cry
from the years gone by…you said I could 'call you
whenever I wanted.' I fear I have abused it. If so, it is only
because I love you.

Dear Lady
Perhaps true love never/runs smooth—but since I love you
truly, this 'pin'
tries to tell you I am
Your devoted man.

"He repeatedly makes references to "jungle money" and "pin," code words for money that J. Howard gave to Lady Walker. "Pin" was a regular payment made on a consistent and timely basis, "Jungle money" was a payment for her own pleasure, and "big kills" were larger sums given sporadically to Lady Walker.

"J. Howard also gave Lady Walker enormous amounts of jewelry, including more than $1 million purchased from Harry Winston and Neiman Marcus, the same stores where he would subsequently buy jewelry for Vickie.

"At one point, J. Howard sent Lady Walker the Koch Industries prospectus in an apparent attempt to impress her with his wealth. The front of the first page reads,

For Lady-
The Crown jewels
J. Howard.

"This pattern of giving money, and even the terms that J. Howard used, is the same pattern that Vickie describes of J. Howard's pursuit of her a decade later. Lavish jewelry, regular payments of money, and sporadic gifts ushered these bar dancers into J. Howard's life.

"Apparently, it was extremely lucrative to have an affair with J. Howard. J. Howard spent approximately $2 million a year on Lady Walker, which is approximately the same amount of money he spent each year on Vickie when he pursued her a decade later.

"J. Howard's statement that 'men in love do stupid things and I was sure guilty' is accurate. In J. Howard's case, it was a consistent pattern.

"J. Howard's affair with Lady Walker continued uninterrupted until she died suddenly as a result of complications from facelift surgery on July 9, 1991 at the age of fifty-one. The effect of her death on J. Howard was initially described by him as the most tragic thing that ever happened to him.

"Ironically, shortly after Lady Walker's death, J. Howard discovered that she had betrayed their relationship and had been living with another, much younger, man during most of their affair. Outrage drove J. Howard to sue her estate in January 1992 seeking the return of almost $15,000,000 in gifts that J. Howard had given Lady Walker. J. Howard accused Lady Walker of fraud, claiming she received kickbacks from merchants after the items were purchased and the merchants had charged J. Howard's account."

When he came under question by the Internal Revenue Service, it was calculated that he had given Lady Walker gifts and cash valued between $12 million and $14 million, without paying gift tax. Throughout his life, J. Howard repeatedly attempted to avoid paying taxes altogether and always sought to find ways to get out of it.

He fought against all kinds of tax. "He argued against the inheritance tax provisions, claiming that being forced to pay estate and income taxes was 'double taxation,' while at the same time he avoided paying substantial income taxes by: writing off as business expenses the gifts to his paramours Lady Walker and Vickie, whom he claimed were consultants."

He financed his lifestyle by taking a line of credit against his stock portfolio, the proceeds of which were not taxable income, and he hid and manipulated his assets in aggressive accounting gimmicks. Isn't it funny how the poor get drained when it comes to taxes and the rich can afford to find ways to avoid paying up? In other words: The poor get poorer and the rich, richer.

J. Howard found sneaky loopholes to bypass gift tax and, during litigation, it was discovered that he had discovered a way to use his affair with Lady Walker to his advantage. "J. Howard took the unlikely position that his 'pin' payments to Lady Walker were consulting fees. At one point, he suggested that she receive a salary of $1 million per year to handle his public relations work. Lady Walker also served on the MPI Board of Directors. When questioned about her functions, he replied, 'I guess she was a Director—never active—she never undertook anything as a Director.'"

He not only tried to escape gift taxes this way, but it is likely that he deducted his payments to Lady Walker from his income tax returns. He was trying to funnel untaxed money through a stripper! The IRS tax audits are still being litigated.

J. Howard's success earned him a ranking in *Forbes Magazine* as one of the four hundred wealthiest men in America, and the wealthiest man in Texas, but he did not like the publicity that this high ranking brought. What worried J. Howard more than publicity was the spotlight that it shined on his wealth. Being named as one of the richest men in the country was likely to attract the attention of the IRS, as well as every charity organization in the country.

However, when he met Vickie, all this changed. At the time he was introduced to her in a strip bar, he was at rock bottom. His morale was so low that, no matter how much international notoriety they would attract as a couple, he still incessantly begged for more attention from Anna!

Vickie was not the first stripper he had courted and, judging by his character, neither was Lady Diane Walker. He had sleazy affairs throughout his life and, in my opinion, the Old Man and my sister deserved each other.

They both had a history of scandal and tragedy. J. Howard divorced his first wife and outlived his second wife and mistress. The former died of Alzheimer's disease, while the latter died because of complications from plastic surgery—How bizarre is that? He then married a stripper sixty-three years younger than him. He disinherited his older son, entrusting his younger son, Pierce, with his estate. He fired his loyal family attorney in favor of another, Edwin Hunter, a liar, who conspired with Pierce to prevent him from having access to his own funds. He died, leaving his son and wife to fight over his $1.6 billion estate. Then, completely out of the blue, his only heir died from an infection at the age of sixty-seven—in the middle of an unfinished ten-year-long court battle. Not even the writers for *Dallas* could have concocted a more scandalous story line.

CHAPTER 7

A FAIRY TALE WEDDING

"He wanted to make me happy.
My wish was his command."

—ANNA NICOLE SMITH ON
J. HOWARD MARSHALL II

*I*n one of the strangest weddings the world had ever seen, the stunning twenty-six-year-old blonde with a massive chest, married wheelchair-bound billionaire, J. Howard Marshall, aged eighty-nine.

As soon as Anna met J. Howard, she told him she wanted to focus on her career. She declined his daily marriage proposals under the pretext that she wanted to make a name for herself first and Marshall therefore did everything he could to help her fulfill her ambitions. He subsidized her modeling and acting career while she went off without him. In the years leading up to their wedding, they never lived together and, even once they were married, it was a rarity for Anna to spend the night under the same roof as her husband.

Anna kept pushing back the wedding so that she could allow herself enough time to seduce the Old Man into leaving her his estate. She waited three years before giving in and did everything in her power to make him rewrite his will and abandon any form of prenuptial agreement. However, in order to beat Pierce to the will she would have to keep his son out of the picture.

J. Howard's wedding to Anna Nicole was held in secret because it would have been sabotaged if Pierce had found out. When J. Howard finally did convince Anna Nicole to take his hand, they left it to the last minute before announcing their plans. She gave her aunt just three days to arrange the entire event. "She wanted a heart-shaped cake; it had to be three-tiered," Elaine Tabers revealed. "It was just the wedding party. J. Howard did not want [his family] there." Aunt Elaine and her husband were there to take videotapes of the ceremony and help organize the event.

On June 27, 1994, J. Howard married Vickie at a ceremony in Houston. The wedding was attended by J. Howard's secretary, Eyvonne Scurlock, one of his nurses, Charlotte Fade, and Vickie's aunt and uncle. Arnold Wyche, J. Howard's driver, brought J. Howard to the ceremony but did not attend. Virgie, Aunt Kay and Anna's cousins were not invited; nor was J. Howard's son, E. Pierce.

They were married at the White Dove Wedding Chapel, and *everything*, including the guests' outfits, was white. Anna looked beautiful but slightly comical, bursting out of her puffy fairy-tale wedding dress; Daniel, the ring bearer, was dressed in a white tuxedo; and J. Howard was rolled in on his wheelchair, dressed in white from hair to shoe. Anna walked up the aisle on white rose buds to the song "Tonight I celebrate my love for you," and at the end of the ceremony two white doves were set free.

The afternoon of the wedding, Vickie informed J. Howard that she had to leave that day for Greece to model at a photo session. She literally left her husband at the altar and flew off for Greece with her then-bodyguard/lover, Pierre DeJean.

J. Howard was devastated that Vickie had abandoned him on their wedding night. He was crying at home and Aunt Elaine and Uncle Melvin were left to comfort him. Uncle Melvin was very close to J. Howard. Considering the fact that Anna typically escaped as soon as she could, they spent a lot of time together without her. Melvin would always try to reassure J. Howard that Anna was not after his money and that she cared for him but had to go and do her own thing. He tried to explain to J. Howard that she wanted to make a career. She was young and it was not in her character to stay at home and play housewife.

After the ceremony, Anna asked Aunt Elaine to call me and tell me that she had gotten married. Aunt Elaine called me the next day and said "You won't believe this; your crazy sister married the Old Man yesterday." I wasn't surprised because my sister was capable of anything bizarre. She apologized that I was not invited. She said that the couple did not want to tell anyone in case it leaked to Pierce. At that time I was living in New Mexico and I sent Anna a letter of congratulations. She returned this gesture when I got married a few years later.

Before Anna and J. Howard set a date for the wedding, they went on a pre-honeymoon to Bali. They left a month before the actual wedding, as it was the only time that J. Howard could sneak off for a long time with the hope that his son, E. Pierce Marshall, would not notice. No one knew that they were engaged and the date for the wedding had not yet been set. Anna had already stalled getting married for years and insisted on this pre-honeymoon with J. Howard so that she could have one last chance at buttering him up. She wanted to show J. Howard what a wonderful wife she could be so that he would do away with any sort of prenuptial agreement.

My sister was swaying the Old Man constantly. Even though he repeatedly begged her to marry him and seemed to be the one chasing her, she was really manipulating him the entire time. It was not enough that he wanted to marry her; she wanted him to hand over his entire estate too. She pulled out all the stops. Did she love him? Maybe in her own way, but it was all about the financial support he was able to offer.

However, her plan backfired. Pierce was one step ahead of the game. Despite all her efforts, two weeks after she became J. Howard's wife, Pierce had his father sign a new will leaving her none of his estate. Anna is not one to give up without a fight though; her entire relationship with J. Howard was centered on his will. From the very first moment she met him to the day he died, Anna had no reservations in that department.

On their romantic trip to Bali, Anna took her Aunt Elaine and Uncle Melvin with her. They were there to be at Anna's beck and call and Anna made them videotape a lot of the goings on. On the tape recording it shows Anna playing in the pool naked with her hair braided in cornrows. She was trying to be completely sexy for J. Howard, who watched from his wheelchair on the sideline. Aunt Elaine is sitting nearby and her husband, Uncle Melvin, is rolling the tape. It didn't seem to bother Anna at all that she was naked and made most of the people around her uncomfortable.

Later it shows them having drinks and talking at a table outside. J. Howard is sitting by Anna wearing a straw hat and sunglasses. He starts singing a ding-a-ling song to her, showing us how perverted he actually was. Anna tries to seem amused but you can tell she's not. Then she says, laughing, "he loves to sing to me," as if this would conceal her disgust.

During the holiday, Anna spent more time with J. Howard than she ever had or ever would again. The videotape portrays their relationship to be a joke but Anna was clever to make sure their interactions were filmed and could be used as evidence later on.

On the same trip, Aunt Elaine recalls Anna shrieking from the bedroom for someone to help her. Aunt Elaine ran to see what was happening and found J. Howard in a state on the bed. His pajamas had been ripped open and his buttons were scattered on the floor. His hair was disheveled and he looked pale and completely helpless. Vickie had obviously been trying to excite him with one of her kinky shows but Aunt Elaine did not ask any questions. She was shocked by his appearance and did not want to know any of the details. She could already guess. Instead, she was left to dress J. Howard and put him to bed, while Anna went out.

Her live-in aunt and uncle witnessed many of her antics but remained removed. Elaine and Melvin are very religious. Aunt Elaine goes on missionary retreats as often as she can; she is devoted to her faith. You can therefore imagine what it was like for her and her husband to deal with Anna on a permanent basis. Around the time Anna was starting to make a name for herself, she asked Aunt Elaine to be her personal assistant. She paid Elaine and Melvin to live at and run her ranch. Their job also entailed going on trips with her and making sure she had all her needs seen to twenty-four-seven.

After too many years of abuse they had had it. They moved out of the ranch and got their own house. Anna was too much for them to deal with around the clock. She always wanted her own way and had a tantrum until she got it. She would scream at her relatives for no apparent reason and, after a while, they couldn't take it anymore. They needed their own lives instead of living through hers.

Anna was very childish when they went their separate ways. After they moved out, Aunt Elaine told me that Anna had accused them of stealing around $20,000 from her. She was very hurt by this, especially after all they had put up with and sacrificed for their niece. Aunt Elaine told Anna that if they needed the money that badly they would have just asked for it. But they were very modest people. They didn't need more than Anna was paying them. They were not financially strapped and absolutely did not take the money. Anna said she still did not believe them but it was all a game to her. Her resentment towards them was undoubtedly because they had quit before she could fire them.

Vickie was always traveling and misplacing stuff along the way. She would lose jewelry and clothes and immediately accuse someone else. Every time it would turn out that she had misplaced whatever it was, but she had to find some one other than herself to blame. She didn't care what she put her friends and family through by making these false accusations.

Even in court she lied, saying she did not have all her millions of dollars worth of gifts any longer because they had been stolen. She testified that, "Although it is commonly known that my husband gave me a large amount of jewelry that cost him several million dollars, all of this jewelry has been stolen from me over the past eighteen months, I suspect by relatives, former bodyguards, former friends, and my son's former nanny. The only jewelry I have left are the two pieces I wear constantly—my wedding ring and my inexpensive watch."

Asked to explain how she managed to lose a king's ransom in jewelry, Vickie answered, "I used to be a real ditz." Even though this statement is clearly true, it is impossible to lose that much jewelry. It certainly wasn't all stolen, despite her offensive accusations. Once she went on a trip to Florida and when she got back all her rings were missing. Vickie cried hysterically and blamed anyone in sight. She called up Aunt Elaine, and accused her of stealing them. She screamed that she had gone away for a few days and now that she was back all her jewelry had disappeared. Before she had left, Aunt Elaine had seen her put them in her jewelry box when she was clearing up and that's exactly where they still were.

During his court battle with Anna, Pierce Marshall subpoenaed Elaine and Melvin to court. They had traveled and lived with Vickie and knew almost everything about her. Pierce had also got wind of the videotapes in which she was filmed harassing J. Howard about his will. The courts were informed that these tapes existed and told Aunt Elaine she had to produce them as evidence. Anna knew about this and freaked out, as, for obvious reasons, she did not want the tapes to be shown. However, luckily for her, the tapes had been lost and Aunt Elaine couldn't find them.

Even though Elaine and Melvin had been subpoenaed and were forced by law to go and give testimony, Anna did not believe them. She accused them of going behind her back and lying about her. She screamed that she could not believe they could be bought so easily by her opposition. She would call them at all hours of the day and curse at them and tell them she hated them.

They came to the end of their tether. Elaine and Melvin had done nothing wrong and yet they were being woken up and harassed incessantly. They told Anna not to call them anymore; they wanted nothing more to do with her. But she ignored their pleas and eventually they had to get their number changed and unlisted so that Anna could no longer track them down.

Last year, Uncle Melvin became seriously ill and, for the first time, inquired into selling stories about Anna. At this point, Elaine had became so disenchanted with Vickie and, with Melvin having heart problems, she wanted to know how much money she could make off of pictures of Vickie and the Old Man. Aunt Elaine had the pictures she had taken of Vickie after she had had lipo-suction. She had all the good stuff.

The most valuable possession Elaine had was the videotape that featured J. Howard's so-called last will and testament. This was why E. Pierce had subpoenaed Elaine and why Anna had become so frantic that it might be held against her in court. However, Elaine could never find the videotape; it went missing for thirteen years. Then one day, after Hurricane Katrina, Elaine phoned me up and told me that after all these years she had found the tape of the honeymoon.

As soon as she had heard Hurricane Katrina was coming, Elaine had packed everything she could. She put all the boxes from the attic and everything else in the house into her car and drove from Liberty to Mexia, Texas with Melvin. They stayed there for a week and when they got back she unpacked all the boxes and started rearranging her house. While she was sorting through her things she found about a thousand photos of Anna from the time they had spent living together. Then she went through her laundry basket in her attic and found the videotape that Melvin had recorded of the pre-honeymoon. She was so excited she called me up.

There was a huge buzz when the media got wind that the tape had been found. She had been looking for it for years as she had wanted to make some money in aid of Uncle Melvin's poor health. There was a lot of pressure for her to find the other tape also and so she began to search frantically for days. There were a lot of videotapes and so she had to root through them all and play bits on the video-recorder, as they were not labeled properly. Then two weeks later, while we were on the phone, she was looking through the same pile of stuff and the videotape fell out of one of the bags. We were like, "you don't think it could be *the* tape? The one with the will?" I told her to pop it in so I stayed on the phone with Elaine while Melvin put it in the player.

The first thing that came on was Anna driving a four-wheeler like a mad woman with her husband on the back. Elaine knew that this had happened at Christmas and so she tried to rewind it to the beginning but the VCR wouldn't let her. It was an old VCR player as everyone uses DVDs nowadays and so we had to wait before we could find out if the right footage was at the beginning.

Elaine and Melvin went to Wal-Mart to buy a VCR and brought it over to my house. We had to go to the airport first to pick up a British journalist from *Splash News*. My publicist, Karen Ammond, had set up a meeting between me and the same journalist the previous year, as *Splash* had wanted to do a story on me. The journalist had flown to Texas to interview me and, although it never worked out, I became friends with him. I phoned him for Elaine and told him about the tapes and *Splash* set up a deal with her for the rights to the video and pictures.

Once we picked him up we all went to my house: Elaine, the journalist and I, to watch the tapes. We all sat on my bed and watched Anna's manipulative tactics. I recall *Splash News* paid Elaine $1,000 up front, but it took her ages to get the rest of the payment; that is if she ever got it at all.

Splash made network deals with *ABC News* and *Extra* for five-figure numbers for Elaine's story, but all the stations expected me to be included in the package. *Splash* implied that they wanted to interview me too, but when it came down to it, Elaine was all they got.

I knew how to negotiate with the press and Elaine was skeptical about the whole ordeal; she wanted me to be there to support her and so I went along with her to the hotel where she was being interviewed. When I arrived at the Four Seasons Hotel in downtown Houston, I phoned up to the room to see if Elaine was there yet. The producer from *ABC Primetime* saw me and became really excited that I had agreed to do the interview. She was especially nice to me, as she obviously wanted me to dish the dirt on Anna. Then I told her I was not doing the interview, it was just Elaine, and she got really angry because she had been promised something she couldn't have.

I could have easily negotiated a percentage of the $50,000 or so for myself and I wanted to go on *ABC News* as I regard them highly. I did not want to appear rude by passing on their offer, but I said no anyway. It was Elaine's story and her deal, and I reassured myself that it would all come back to me in the end if I did the right thing. ABC went ahead with the interview with Elaine, but they were really rude to her and rushed through the questions to get them over and done with.

Elaine was also really worried that Anna would retaliate and attack her and Melvin for selling her story. These tapes obviously didn't show Anna in the best light and Elaine was scared of her; she had lived with her niece and knew what she was capable of. I told Elaine to blame me if it made things easier for her; I knew Anna would probably accuse me anyway, as she had frequently announced that I had sold her out, even though at that time I hadn't sold my story to a single magazine. Following my instructions, Elaine told *Extra* that it was because of me that the story about the tapes had leaked and so of course Anna tried to get revenge.

When the story came out, Anna couldn't keep quiet for a minute. She immediately told her side of the story to *Extra* but it was never broadcast. The only reason I know the show was recorded is because the producer personally called me up and asked me to talk about the tapes. He told me that Anna had given them an interview and they wanted to include my side of the story. When I refused, he offered me more and more money, but I didn't give in.

Anna was then in the middle of her appeal to the Supreme Court in her effort to obtain hundreds of millions of dollars from her deceased husband, J. Howard Marshall, and her lawyers wanted her to appear professional. The only way that this could be achieved was by silencing Anna and so she ended up stopping *Extra* from using her interview. I don't know whether a gag order had been put on her by the Supreme Court, or she had simply made a deal with the producers. Whatever the reason, her lawyers made sure the interview was pulled and nothing further was said on the subject. It must have been hard for her to keep quiet with the whole world having access to the tapes of her, but it was more important for her to be taken seriously in court.

The media was expecting this story to blow up into a huge scandal but, because Anna could not respond, it died pretty quickly. I refused to talk and, by herself, Elaine could not stay in the headlines for very long. However, now that the tapes have been found, maybe they will be used as evidence in the next round of court hearings for Dannielynn's claim to the estate.

CHAPTER 8

DONNA AND THE MEDIA

From the very beginning of our relationship, the English journalist from *Splash* was always trying to come on to me. For the sake of his marriage, I will call him "John" (not his real name). In July 2005, before anything sexual happened between us, I got the chance to go to Miami where he lived. We kept trying to meet up, but we constantly had different obligations and never got to spend time together.

One night he went to a club on the strip—near the Coconut Grove Hotel, where I was staying in Miami—and waited for me there with some friends. My girlfriend, April, and I had hired a big van for ourselves and the kids so that we could get around while we were in Florida. While he was waiting for us, April and I got stuck in stand-still traffic. There was a hurricane scare in Key West and the whole area was being evacuated so we were held up. John was completely drunk and kept calling me over and over again, begging me to meet him there. He told me he had loved me since the first time he met me and when I told him that it was ridiculous he started crying. John would drunk-dial me all the time and even to this day he sometimes calls me when he has had too much to drink.

I didn't get to meet him that night, but just before we left Florida, April, the kids and I drove from Miami to Orlando so that the journalist and I could spend my last night there together. I had gone all that way hoping to hook up with him, and I was going to make damn sure it happened.

It was the day the space shuttle was supposed to launch from the Kennedy Space Center—which is situated right by Orlando—and so there were press everywhere and all the hotels in the vicinity were booked up. We all ended up having to stay in John's hotel suite. There were two rooms so it was okay for all of us to share.

The hotel where he had been put up was full of journalists and photographers. This was around the time that Anna told the world that I was a "user-loser," feeding off of her fame and money and that I would do anything for my fifteen minutes in the limelight. I refused to respond to these accusations, which annoyed her and made her lash out even more. I therefore felt particularly insecure about being in a hotel with a married man, while surrounded by the press who all wanted my story. I had just come to Florida to get away from being harassed and I ended up in a hotel full of journalists.

The next thing I found out was that Anna was in Orlando, too. Now I knew that that was too much of a coincidence to begin with and then, confirming my gut feeling, John's boss rang his room and asked him to do an interview with Anna. Anna had specifically said that she would only do an interview with *Splash* if John would do it that day. She would not do it with anyone else. There was obviously something going on. Somehow it must have leaked to Anna that romance was kindling between us and she had specifically requested him to get at me. I wanted John to do it. I was curious to see what she wanted, but he wouldn't go for it. It sounded too suspicious for him and he thought that his marriage might be at stake if he messed with Anna. He was probably right.

By the time Aunt Elaine had found the videotapes in November 2005, John and I were having a full-blown affair so I let him stay at my house for the weekend. When we were apart, he would often send me text messages, telling me that he was in love with me. He would use any excuse to come to Montgomery County to see me. Even after he saw the videotapes, he would say that he needed to interview Elaine again and he would fly over to see me instead.

Splash made a deal with Vickie's mother, Virgie, at the same time as Elaine. She had never before done any interviews about her daughter, but they persuaded her to sign a contract stating that she would start doing interviews about Anna exclusively with them. It is not publicly known, but it was before Daniel died that Virgie contractually obligated herself to talk about Anna. However, it was mainly after her grandson's death that Virgie's interviews were aired everywhere, making it appear as if she was selling out on the unfortunate turn of events.

Virgie hated me and knew that Elaine and I were very close. We would talk for up to five hours a day, especially while we were negotiating all the press deals for her. Even though I have tried to help Virgie and always stuck up for her, to this day she does not want anything to do with me. When *Splash* wanted her to sign the deal with them, she would only agree if Elaine would stop speaking to me. After I set up the whole thing for both Elaine and Virgie with *Splash*, Aunt Elaine sided with Virgie and has since refused to speak to me.

I stopped seeing John. He would keep calling and texting me inappropriate messages, but I knew he was married and didn't want to pursue a relationship with him. After the weekend when we played the videotape, I didn't let him stay with me anymore. He would still come to Texas, but he would stay in a hotel and beg me to come and visit him there. By this point, I was married to Robert and he had somehow read the provocative texts on my phone. He threatened to beat up John if he came near me or my house so there was no way I could have him over. I was forced to sneak off to meet him but nothing intimate ever happened between us again.

After Elaine stopped talking to me, I wanted to find out if the rumors about J. Howard's sperm being frozen were true. Aunt Elaine had told John and me previously where J. Howard had had his sperm tested; after all, Uncle Melvin had accompanied him. I couldn't remember exactly where she had said it was and so I asked John, as he was there when Elaine told us. He couldn't remember either, so I told him to call Elaine and find out.

I kept calling John and asking him what he had found out about the sperm being frozen, but he said that he couldn't get hold of Elaine. He kept making up lies that he didn't know anything, even though I knew that he had spoken to Elaine since. John was annoyed with me because *Splash* wanted an exclusive deal with me, but I did not want to meet with them or sign a contract. They didn't want to tell me anything anyway because they knew I would not do a story exclusively with them.

It really infuriated me because John was texting and calling me at every given opportunity. I had set up the meeting with Elaine for him and supplied all the information I could when he needed it but when I wanted to know what he had uncovered, he wouldn't tell me. So I texted him back and wrote, "Well if you don't want to give me the info, I'm sure your wife will!" Within thirty seconds he called me back and begged me not to go to his wife. Just for the record, I would never go to his wife. Telling on him would be like giving myself away and I would never intentionally jeopardize a marriage.

I was only threatening him so he would tell me where the sperm bank is. John was obviously really freaked out though because he continued to text me every five minutes, insisting that he didn't know anything and that I shouldn't go to his wife—even when I knew he was lying. For the record, even though I know J. Howard was fertile when he married Anna, the rumor that he got his sperm frozen is purely speculative. But then again, after all these years, I knew that where my sister was concerned, anything was possible.

CHAPTER 9

THE PHANTOM WIFE

*The people who are
absent are the ideal;
those who are present seem
to be quite commonplace.*

—JOHANN WOLFGANG VON GOETHE

*A*nna Nicole saw to it that she and her husband spent very little time together. In fact, they never lived together full time and, when they got together, she made sure there was always an excuse to leave. J. Howard's office manager testified that a log was kept of Vickie's comings and goings and the time they spent together. According to this log they spent a total of seventeen days together between June 27, 1994 and December 31, 1994. This means that during the first six months of their marriage they spent just a little over two weeks in each other's company!

Nobody in Hollywood seemed to care that she couldn't act. Following her appearances in a series of *Playboy* video documentaries, she began a film and television career, with a bit part as Za-Za in Ethan and Joel Coen's comedy *The Hudsucker*

Proxy, starring Tim Robbins, Jennifer Jason Leigh and Paul Newman. Za-Za is the stunning date who flitters from one successful man to the next. Even though her role consisted of only one line and two short cameo scenes, her beauty was accentuated on screen.

This led to a larger part in the action comedy *Naked Gun 33 1/3: The Final Insult*, starring Leslie Nielson, Priscilla Presley and George Kennedy. Her role as Tanya Peters earned the aspiring actress the Razzie award for being the worst new star. This did not deter Anna though, and the subsequent year she starred as Colette Dubois/Vickie Linn in the action thriller *To the Limit*, with Joey Travolta.

In the August 22, 1994 edition of the *New York* magazine, Vickie was used as the cover girl for an article called "White Trash Nation." She appeared in the photo squatting down eating chips, dressed in a concealed short skirt and white cowboy boots. In October 1994, her lawyer initiated a five-million-dollar lawsuit against the magazine claiming that the photo used was unauthorized and the article had damaged her reputation.

It seems strange for her to emphatically denounce the association with trailer-park trash, when at other times she would play up to the image. It's not as if Anna took herself seriously on a regular basis—later, she would star in a self-mocking reality show—but, in this case, Anna was not happy with her portrayal. Somehow my sister always managed to make something out of nothing and, in the end, they paid her about $100,000 to settle the suit out of court. However, that didn't stop others.

Once a year, *Texas Monthly* issues what it calls its "Bum Steer Awards." According to the magazine, it is read by over 2,500,000 people every month—that is one out of every seven Texan adults. The annual Bum Steer Awards are issued to highlight events that have led to the state's downfall and to ridicule politicians and other personalities from the previous year whose bizarre antics they feel should be given recognition. And you know who was a winner of 1995….

The *Monthly* had plenty of reason, they said, to award Vickie with the less-than-prestigious honor. They wrote:

"THE ECONOMY DIDN'T GO BUST IN 1995, BUT PRACTICALLY EVERYTHING ELSE DID…. When it comes to going bust, however, few can match Anna Nicole Smith. Take the outfit the 28-year-old model wore to the funeral of her 90-year-old hubby, Houston oil tycoon J. Howard Marshal, II: *People* described it as 'a white gown with its neckline at half mast.' Buxom she may be, but bucksome she isn't…."

That should be enough to keep anybody busy for a year, but Anna Nicole still found time to celebrate a Planet Hollywood restaurant opening in San Diego by joining part-owner Bruce Willis on stage—and pop out of her dress; lose a lawsuit to a former housekeeper, who accused her of sexual harassment; win a settlement from *New York* magazine over an unflattering cover photo that showed her gobbling junk food for its "White Trash Nation" issue; and cause a stir at the Academy Awards, which she attended with her *To The Limit* co-star, Branscom Richmond. For the event, she dressed in an unflattering skintight dress, which served only to accentuate her sudden weight gain. The photos of Anna, larger than she'd ever been before, made the news headline the following day. With such credentials, who else could be our Bum Steer of the Year but Anna Nicole Smith?

Even when she was in Texas, she often didn't let J. Howard know. The Old Man didn't see much of her, but seemed to accept it as part of the bargain. Occasionally Anna put in an appearance, danced naked for him, and provided him with sexual gratification.

Meanwhile, E. Pierce was desperately conspiring with his father's new attorney to cut Vickie off from his father. It had already been several years since she began taking everything she could get her hands on from the Old Man and Pierce did not want his inheritance jeopardized. His father was giving the gold-digger an allowance as well as paying all her bills. He had bought her a townhouse, a Toyota Celica, and a Mercedes-Benz. He had also lavished her with $10,000 gowns that could only be worn once and jewelry purchases that exceeded $2 million.

One of the things I'll never forget was Vickie's hunger for money and material objects. Once, she wanted yet another exorbitant piece of jewelry from J. Howard and it would cost him a bit over a million dollars. The Old Man, while filthy rich, had to be careful because E. Pierce was watching his spending like a hawk, especially with "Miss Cleavage" around.

She really wanted this necklace and she baby-talked the Old Man till it was disgusting. She would say to me, "Come on Donna you gotta meet him and sit on his lap, he'd love that." Like hell, I was going to sit on the old guy's lap and play lap dog for my sister.

Anyway, Vickie was relentless and got the Old Man to take her to Rodeo Drive in Beverly Hills, California. Now remember, in E. Pierce's eyes, my sister was nothing more than a gold-digging, untrustworthy bimbo and so he had tied up a lot of the Old Man's money. Don't get me wrong, the Old Man still carried a cache of credit cards and a checkbook, but large sums of cash were not readily at his disposal.

Finally, the Old Man relented and wrote a check for more than a million dollars so that Vickie could get the necklace. Then, to Vickie's absolute horror, the million-dollar check bounced! The store began calling, imploring Vickie to return the necklace. Even J. Howard called trying to get Vickie to give back the necklace. The Old Man asked Aunt Elaine to tell her to return it, but she wouldn't. She flat out refused to give the necklace back. The Old Man said the store was angling to have him locked up for fraud and a bounced check if she didn't return the necklace. David, Elaine, Melvin, and Virgie's brother pleaded with Vickie to give it back but she kept saying it was rightfully hers. If her "Paw-Paw," as she sometimes called the Old Man, was going to jail, so be it.

Eventually, the Old Man made up some story to E. Pierce and got the dough to settle the account with the store. I think because of his age, J. Howard didn't care too much about what had happened as long as it was taken care of and as long as Vickie would be there to wheel him around. His office personnel stated that Anna was spending five to six figures a month on his credit card. If she did not get what she wanted, she would threaten him. "I'm going into the hospital," Vickie has been quoted as saying. "They're going to cut off my breast, I have cancer."

So much of my sister's life with J. Howard has been told, but not many people knew how she treated the Old Man. People obviously guessed and speculated but they did not know the extent of how much she used him.

Steve Jakubowski calculated what Vickie's funds accumulated to: "Over time, J. Howard purchased jewelry for Vickie's use costing in excess of $4 million. On September 16, 1992, J. Howard purchased a ranch in Tomball, Texas, for Vickie's use.... J. Howard also purchased a home for her in Houston.... Because Vickie spent a great deal of time in Los Angeles, J. Howard leased a home for her there and later he purchased a different home for her in LA, too (the "Brentwood House"). In 1992 he purchased a new Mercedes for her use.... In addition to these gifts, J. Howard promoted Vickie's career as a *Playboy* Playmate and international model. He bought her expensive clothing and gave her cash."

This is not even the extent of her desires; with Anna there were no limits. When Anna arrived in Los Angeles, she demanded to live in the same Bentwood house that her idol, Marilyn Monroe, had once lived and died in and so, naturally, that was where she moved to. The house on Helena Street had a huge crack and would have been too expensive to renovate and so J. Howard bought her another house instead.

Later, in the court case between Anna Nicole and J. Howard's son, the jury was informed that during their entire relationship J. Howard Marshall gave his wife:

$69,000 for her modeling and acting clothes

$804,000 for jewelry

$597,000 for her L.A. house

$82,000 for her Mercedes

$439,000 for miscellaneous spendings

$693,000 for the ranch

$230,000 for the ranch furnishings

This adds up to a whopping total of $6,607,000, but still Anna wanted more—she wanted total control over his estate.

Prior to their marriage, J. Howard and Anna Nicole were often apart. Although she would call him frequently for money, she rarely visited him. Vickie referred to J. Howard as "Paw Paw." In public, she told others that he was her grandfather. J. Howard would spontaneously fly to Los Angeles or New York to visit her. Prior to their marriage, during one of his trips to Los Angeles to visit her, Vickie claimed to have injured her leg and, during his stay, spent much of the time in bed wearing a cast.

However, while J. Howard was taking a nap, his nurse, Betty Harding, came across Vickie in another room with the cast off and her arms and legs embraced around her housekeeper, giggling and rubbing noses. Later on, during the visit, J. Howard went shopping with Nurse Harding to purchase jewelry for Vickie. When they returned with the jewelry, Vickie demanded to see the receipt and complained that J. Howard had not spent enough money on the purchase. J. Howard returned to the store to buy her some more expensive jewelry.

During a trip to New York, J. Howard waited in his hotel for several days only to have Vickie grace him with her presence for a total of thirty minutes. Just before he was scheduled to leave, Vickie asked that he meet her at an exclusive jewelry store, Harry

Winston. When J. Howard arrived at the store and met with Vickie, he was not interested in shopping. Vickie gave him a Valium, leaving him incoherent and drooling in his wheelchair. While he was not mentally present, she had him buy her a sixteen-carat diamond engagement ring: the store's record-breaking purchase mentioned before. On the return trip to Houston, J. Howard had heart palpitations and Harding was concerned that, as a result of the Valium, J. Howard might have died.

During the summer of 1994, members of J. Howard's staff learned that Vickie's "bodyguard," Pierre DeJean, had a record of multiple felony convictions. Just prior to her marriage to J. Howard, Vickie "lost" much of the jewelry that J. Howard had given her, including her engagement ring. She filed a police report in Los Angeles, claiming the property had been stolen. Contradicting her claim, she also asserted that she had given the jewelry to DeJean. Further contradicting her claim, she said that she had left the jewelry in a bag in a cab. The jewelry has never been recovered and the police did not believe Vickie's story, stating: "the report of lost jewelry is unfounded." After this incident they informed Vickie that DeJean had a long-standing felony record, but she did nothing about it. In fact, later in court she claimed that she had never been told anything about her bodyguard's criminal history, even though that was obviously untrue.

Perhaps Anna refused to acknowledge Pierre DeJean's history because she was having an affair with him. He insists that they had a long-term relationship even though she denied it all. He was violent towards her and once beat her so hard he nearly knocked out her front teeth. He claimed it was because she had cheated on him, even though according to her they were never romantically involved in the first place. When she finally did end up firing him, he stole everything of hers on his way out. He took all her important documents: her marriage certificate, photos of her family and Daniel, Daniel's things, and he almost cleaned out all the jewelry J. Howard had given her. He even stole the only other copy of the video Melvin had recorded of J. Howard's will. I guess he thought that he would be able to make a lot of money by selling out on Anna.

With DeJean around, E. Pierce Marshall had detectives hired to follow the three of them. In court he claimed he was concerned that, with Pierre DeJean's record, his father might be harmed. However, he only had them tailed during the day, leaving the entire night for the Old Man to be under threat. It was later revealed that the real reason he had them under surveillance was to make sure Anna did not hire a lawyer to rewrite his father's will.

Pierce was not the only one who was concerned about Anna. Everyone who knew J. Howard and had witnessed the way Anna treated him was upset by it, but J. Howard would not listen to their warnings. Although he was very insecure about their relationship, Anna made him feel young. Her crazy personality put life into him and even though she upset him more often than she made him happy, he clung to her. In one respect, J. Howard was using my sister as much as she was using him. He was one exceptionally lucky eighty-nine-year-old man to gain the attention of a beautiful twenty-three-year-old aspiring actress. There are men out there who would have given a lot more to be entertained by Anna.

J. Howard's office manager was forced to keep a log of where she was so he could find her. She often went missing and could not even be reached by phone. J. Howard's driver quoted his employer as saying, "Where is she? I'm in the same house with her. I still can't find her."

In August of 1994, J. Howard flew to Los Angeles with his driver, Wyche, to visit for several days. During the visit, Vickie stayed in her room in bed. When J. Howard suggested that he keep her company, she refused to allow him to lie next to her, stating that he would urinate in the bed. She remained in bed until J. Howard left. When he came to say goodbye, she asked him for money. He gave her his wallet and she took all of his cash, together with a blank check that she had him sign.

On another occasion, J. Howard asked Nurse Harding to take him to visit Vickie at the Tomball Ranch. At the ranch, Vickie asked Harding to leave J. Howard with her. Harding left, and drove to the nearby home of J. Howard's secretary, Eyvonne Scurlock. A short time later, Harding received a phone call from Vickie's aunt requesting that Harding come pick up J. Howard. Harding rushed back to the ranch.

When she arrived, she found Vickie talking with her aunt in a car in the driveway. Harding found J. Howard in the house. His hair was standing up, his clothes were disheveled, and buttons were missing from his shirt. Although he would not tell Harding what happened, he made her promise that she would never again leave him alone with Vickie at her house. He stated that his marriage to Vickie had been a mistake and that Vickie thought of him as a bottomless pit financially. He said he wanted to teach Vickie how to handle her money, but all she wanted to do was spend.

During Christmas of 1994, J. Howard again flew to Los Angeles with Wyche to visit Vickie. When he arrived at her house, Vickie was drunk and having a party with some friends. Soon after his arrival, she sent J. Howard to bed and continued on with her party. On December 23, 1994, J. Howard gave Vickie a stuffed bear with an emerald pendant necklace. She served him breakfast but, because the bacon was raw, he avoided eating it. When she complained that he was not eating the food, he swallowed it. The raw bacon, however, made him sick.

That evening, Vickie insisted that J. Howard go out with her for dinner even though he did not feel well. While they were out, Vickie left J. Howard in his wheelchair in the rain. If it hadn't already become obvious that Vickie was dangerously careless with the frail Old Man, leaving him out in the rain in his wheelchair alone and helpless, it should have sealed the deal for anyone who knew the situation. You had to feel for J. Howard.

Some may judge the old guy for being a dirty old man looking for a little easy pleasing and reasoned that he got what he deserved. But leaving him alone like that was elderly abuse, if not spousal abuse, too.

Afterwards, she went dancing with her bodyguard while Wyche stayed with J. Howard at the house. On Christmas day, Vickie had Wyche take pictures of her and J. Howard. Although they posed together for the photos, she did not spend the day with him.

Before J. Howard left, he gave her an envelope full of cash several inches thick. Obviously this pleased Vickie to no end. She must have been feeling really good about the fact that she had this sugar daddy or, more accurately, sugar great-grand daddy. All she had to do was give him what he wanted—a little strip tease, maybe a lap dance or dry sex was as much as he could handle—and she could get a wad of cash in return.

It All Disappeared as Fast as it Came

> *"I don't want to say he's old,*
> *but yesterday she told him*
> *to act his age—and he died."*
>
> —Jay Leno

*A*fter J. Howard returned to Houston, he became seriously ill and, in January of 1995, was hospitalized. His heart had stopped and he only survived after receiving CPR. While he was in the hospital, Vickie slept in his house with her bodyguard. The bodyguard stayed with her all night and they shared the same bed. Vickie claims that he was there to guard her but it does not take much of an imagination to guess what happened between them that night. J. Howard's housekeeper, Ada Estes, saw Vickie appear just once. She was getting a bowl of cereal and two spoons and was dressed in almost nothing. While her husband was dying in the hospital, Vickie was using his house for one of her many affairs.

Following his stay in the hospital, J. Howard returned to his home in Houston. Vickie had been away, but she flew back to Houston to see him. While at J. Howard's house, she made a special effort to care for him. She knew that the moment she'd been waiting for was fast approaching. Once the Old Man kicked the bucket, she could lay claim to millions from J. Howard's estate. After all, she was his wife.

So, the games began. Vickie decided to cook a little, which she had absolutely no talent in doing. She tried to feed him chicken soup and poor J. Howard had difficulty swallowing it; Vickie didn't care. She tried to stuff it down his throat and caused him to choke. The Old Man lost consciousness and Vickie started screaming and flapped about hysterically. J. Howard's driver, Arnold Wyche, called 911 and relayed their step-by-step instructions to her. In an attempt to resuscitate him, Vickie breathed into the desperate man's mouth once and then pathetically fumbled around, leaving Wyche no alternative but to take over. He continued to give J. Howard mouth-to-mouth until he eventually succeeded in reviving him and the emergency services were able to take him to Spring Branch Hospital for further care. Later, in court, Vickie claimed she saved his life, but it is obvious that if his driver had not been there J. Howard would have choked to death.

Vickie was not entirely stupid and she knew how to get as much as she could at the very last moment. During these last few months of his life, she would often drop in on her husband unexpectedly, bringing someone along to record their last days together. On February 4, 1995, while J. Howard was recovering from the chicken soup incident, Vickie went to visit him at Spring Branch Hospital at 2 a.m.! She brought along a friend of hers, Raymond Martino, a Hollywood filmmaker, to videotape her with her husband. In the middle of the night Vickie woke up her dying husband so that she could secretly record him leaving her his estate.

This was just one of the many occasions she tried to capture the dying man on tape. There is a hospital record that shows Vickie brought along a photographer when she visited her husband. Another time, Vickie brought a tape recorder and sought to tape J. Howard. She climbed into his bed, exposed her breasts and asked J. Howard: "Do you miss your rosebuds?"

On February 22, 1995, J. Howard was admitted to Park Plaza Hospital, where he stayed until March 30, 1995. While there, J. Howard underwent gall bladder surgery. In the spring of 1995, unbeknownst to Vickie, J. Howard was diagnosed with inoperable, terminal stomach cancer.

Many of Anna's visits were supervised. Despite blaming Pierce for not allowing her any alone time with his father, it was in fact J. Howard's caregivers who considered Anna to be a threat to his life. After the chicken soup incident, a nurse caught Anna trying to feed her sick husband solid food when he was barely surviving on a drip. Despite being told it would kill him, Vickie tried repeatedly to bring him solid food, including a barbecued feast.

Vickie also hurt her bed-bound husband emotionally by teasing him with her numerous love interests. She would bring much younger men with her when she visited him at home or in the hospital and she would flirt with them right in his face. This was another reason the nurses believed it was necessary for her visits to be supervised; they felt that her conduct was inappropriate and harmful. After it became clear that J. Howard's morale was being negatively affected, they felt she should no longer be allowed to see him with male company. They also were forced to put restrictions on her visiting hours at the hospital after that time they found her waking up J. Howard at two in the morning.

On May 26, 1995, Vickie visited J. Howard at his home in Texas. It was a visit that was vitally important to her; an opportunity to ensure her position as heiress to his fortune. The old guy may have survived the soup drowning, but he was certainly not going to be in this world for long.

My sister concocted a plan that she knew couldn't fail. She baby-talked the Old Man and then whispered "sweet-nothings" in his ear. She gave the Old Man a "stiffy," knowing that at this point in his life he would go for anything to feel that good.

Yet again, she exposed her breasts to him and asked him to repeat into a tape recorder that he intended to give her half of all of his assets. But things backfired again. This time the Old Man got what he wanted. Vickie was left to beg to no avail—J. Howard refused. He had finally built up the nerve to say no to Anna Nicole.

It was not like J. Howard was unaware of the fact that he was being used. No one could be that oblivious. They both knew it was a marriage of convenience and even though she may have loved him for the financial security he provided her, there was never any attraction to him, sexual or otherwise. According to Elaine, they never once consummated their marriage. J. Howard wasn't even capable of getting it up and perhaps that is why he was content with just touching his wife's boobs. The longest period of time Elaine witnessed them alone together was when Anna screamed for her assistance because all of J. Howard's buttons were undone. God knows what she did to him behind that closed door, but it certainly wasn't sex.

J. Howard knew that Anna was constantly having affairs. She wasn't giving him any and she had to be getting sexual gratification somewhere. J. Howard was even aware of the fact that Anna was living with another man while they were still married. He stuck by her because he liked having a young woman around, even if it was just for brief moments at a time. However, there was no way he would leave all of his fortune to a woman who was unfaithful and mostly absent. No matter how much she twisted him around her little finger or how ill he got, he could never be in bad enough shape to hand over his estate to Anna Nicole.

During the last thirty days of J. Howard's life, Vickie did not once visit her husband in the hospital. Even though he was in and out for months on end and in critical health, Anna stated that no one had told her he was in immediate danger. She lied in court that she had no idea he was dying, when it was clear there was no way it could have been kept from her. To begin with it was all over the media and, if she had even tried to call her husband, it would have been apparent he was not in good condition.

Anna also claimed that Pierce hired bodyguards to stop her from visiting her husband, but there was no way the hospital would have prohibited J. Howard's wife from visiting him if she had tried. The only truth in this is that she was eventually only allowed to see her husband if supervised, but there was a perfectly reasonable explanation. J. Howard was under twenty-four-hour health care so there always had to be someone on guard; the hospital did not want J. Howard to be kept up at 2 a.m. and so they restricted his visiting hours; and they did not want him to sink into depression by having young, good-looking men flaunted in front of him. They thought that it was degrading for Anna to always show up with a video camera, flaunt her fake breasts in his face and try to force him to leave her his estate. Her agenda was so obvious even the hospital staff had had enough.

On August 4, 1995, J. Howard died of heart failure in Houston's Park Plaza Hospital. He was ninety-one years old. The *Houston Chronicle* obituary read: "Mr. Marshall is survived by his third wife, the former Vickie Lynn Hogan (a.k.a. Anna Nicole Smith); son J. Howard Marshall III and daughter-in-law, Elaine T. Marshall and grandsons E. Pierce Marshall, Jr. and Reston L. Marshall of Dallas."

On the night before he died, J. Howard refused Vickie's phone call. He died tired of Vickie and all the shenanigans. He was tempted by Vickie's vibrancy and larger-than-life personality, but he also knew that he had built too much of a legacy and a fortune to allow a stripper from Texas to take advantage of him on his deathbed.

During his marriage, J. Howard called Vickie daily, leaving messages for her to call him. She did not return his calls, contacting him only when she wanted money.

The tables turned at the most inopportune time for Vickie. For if J. Howard had been angry with her a bit earlier, she could have enticed him back. Now, it was too late. Vickie probably didn't realize that her final chance to salvage favors from J. Howard was lost because during the last month of his life, my sister didn't bother to visit him in Houston a single time. Although J. Howard clearly loved Vickie, he ultimately called her "un-teachable." Nurse Harding described J. Howard's experience with Vickie as, "his year of being married to her was just a total long, lonely, frustrating, miserable existence."

Even if all this is not true and the Old Man *was* blinded by love and senility, at this point it no longer mattered what he thought. E. Pierce had been granted legal guardianship over his father since February 16, 1995, permitting him to make any decisions on his father's behalf. E. Pierce immediately went to work, making sure that Anna was kept as far away from his father as possible—her visits were restricted to thirty minutes and supervised by an armed officer, and her excessive allowance was abruptly frozen.

The death of J. Howard Marshall marked the end of a marriage that had lasted a year and a month, and marked the beginning of legal wrangling between Anna Nicole and the Marshall family that would drag on for more than a decade. Grabbing at anything she could, she accused Pierce of letting his father choke to death even though she was not even there to prove it and the hospital records clearly state that he died of a heart attack.

She then fell into a bitter war with J. Howard's family over the funeral arrangements: Anna wanted her husband to be buried in a mausoleum and E. Pierce wanted his father to be cremated. J. Howard II was a Quaker and so eventually it was decided that he would be cremated in accordance with his beliefs. But then Anna and E. Pierce were forced back into court over who would get the ashes. The ugly scrape was only resolved by a Solomon-like compromise: two separate funerals were held and J. Howard's ashes were divided—half to Anna, half to Pierce.

Although they were both held at the same chapel, Geo. H. Lewis & Sons, the two funeral services could not have been more different. The *Houston Chronicle* wrote, "If anyone has any idea of trying to crash the memorial service Sunday, forget it." E. Pierce Marshall saw to it that his guest list included only close family friends and business associates and that the security was as tight as the White House. He wanted the service to be discreet and simple so that the guests could focus on the loss of his father.

Anna Nicole, on the other hand, customized her late husband's funeral arrangements to attract as much attention as possible. She decorated the chapel with a white grand piano and candelabra, then showed up in her backless white wedding dress and laced veil, accessorized with her black lap dog, Beauty. She thought she should add some integrity to what would otherwise have been a private affair by inviting a crowd of journalists to report on the goings on. They were only allowed to watch from outside the chapel as she limited the congregation to the head journalist from *People* magazine and the schlock camera crew from the daily entertainment program *Extra*.

She provided her guests with a flawless performance as the mourning wife. To everyone's surprise she sang, "Wind Beneath My Wings" and then read one line of the Bible before she broke down sobbing. As soon as she confirmed that a video camera was pointed at her, she told the journalists she had invited: "I'm sorry, I can't right now." Just in case this wasn't enough for the journalists to make her headline news the following day, one of her nipples accidentally came out of her bra, guaranteeing her place on the front page of every publication.

The funeral service turned out to be like a Las Vegas wedding with a corpse instead of a husband. Only Anna Nicole Smith could have orchestrated such a charade. In 1995, one woman should have been nominated for best actress in a comedy: "And the Oscar goes to Anna Nicole Smith."

CHAPTER 11

VICKIE TAKES THE STAND

"It's expensive to be me."
—ANNA NICOLE SMITH

Even before J. Howard Marshall II died, the relentless legal battle for his estate had begun. In April 1995, Anna sued E. Pierce for committing fraud in matters concerning his father's 1982 Living Trust and Anna's income. In 1982, E. Pierce had started transferring most of his property to a living trust but all the paperwork was only finalized in July 1994, a couple of weeks after he married Anna Nicole. Once the papers were finalized, the trust was made irrevocable, meaning that it would be almost impossible to make any changes to it.

E. Pierce could legally make decisions on his father's behalf because he was the co-trustee of J. Howard Marshall II's Living Trust, the agent for J. Howard Marshall II under a Power of Attorney dated July 13, 1994, and the Temporary Guardian of J. Howard Marshall II. When the trust was completed in 1994, Anna Nicole was not included in it, nor was she going to receive any money under any of his wills.

Anna blamed E. Pierce for the fact that she had been excluded, saying that he had abused his father's confidence and made changes to the Living Trust and will behind J. Howard's back before it had been finalized. One of Vickie's main arguments was that J. Howard was not in a fit state of mind to have made the trust irrevocable and that it was part of E. Pierce's scheme to exclude her. Anna claimed that the Living Trust was not valid and sought a declaration concerning the ownership of the assets.

It took a mere three days after J. Howard's death for Vickie to make an official claim on his money. Vickie Lynn Marshall filed a petition in the Texas probate court to establish that J. Howard Marshall II died intestate. There was absolutely no way Vickie was going to accept a will that left her nothing and, by claiming that J. Marshall had died "intestate," it meant that it was up to the Texas and Louisiana probate courts to decide who got what. The will, according to Anna's argument, was just a meaningless stack of papers that had been rigged by E. Pierce.

On August 16 1995, Pierce opposed Anna's petition and produced the last will and testament to the probate court to prove that Anna was not included in it. He also filed a counterclaim saying that the trust and will were legally valid.

That is how the case Marshall v. Marshall began, with Vickie demanding half of J. Howard's $1.6 billion estate. J. Howard's other son, James Howard Marshall III, also came forward and claimed that he was promised half of the estate. Even though the elder son had been disinherited and left out of the will, he wanted a share of his father's estate, just like Vickie did. Neither of them had any written evidence and so they both had to rely on J. Howard's oral promises as evidence of his intent. Pierce accused Smith of taking advantage of his father, who reportedly spent millions on her, even though she did not live with him and was allegedly having numerous affairs.

Once the case made the media headlines, E. Pierce Marshall stated to the media: "The public has learned what our family has known for many years that Anna Nicole Smith was cruel to my father and was never his wife in the traditional sense. She worked hard to avoid being with my father but managed to call him constantly demanding more and more money. My father told close associates that the marriage had been a mistake and I believe he would have ended it had he lived."

During the case, E. Pierce and his family kept very low key. Just like their funeral service for J. Howard was removed from the media's scrutiny, so too was their side of the court case against Anna Nicole. Anna was also consistent with her ways. She appealed to the media at every opportunity and it dutifully reported her side of the events to the public.

Factweb.net wrote: "Pierce Marshall is a businessman, family man, husband, father and grandfather who has lived a legal nightmare for the past six years. He lived a quiet and productive life outside the glare of the media spotlight until the death of his father, J. Howard Marshall II, in 1995. While probating his father's will, Pierce Marshall became the target of a hate campaign unprecedented in recent history.

"His father's wife…used her notoriety to go on national television to accuse Pierce Marshall of plotting murder, betraying the father he loved and respected, and attempting to cheat her out of millions of dollars. Aided by a tag team of contingency-fee lawyers circling like vultures and looking for a big kill, Smith and others dragged the Marshall family's good name through the mud as they tried to convince a Houston jury that Smith was promised half of her late husband's estate."

Anna Nicole Smith viciously lashed out at Pierce Marshall even though she admitted she had met him only twice and spoken to him twice by telephone. In one segment of the Howard Stern show, Anna Nicole Smith told the national radio talk show audience that Pierce had cut her off and added, "He's evil, I just can't stand him."

E. Pierce testified: "[Vickie] was attacking me—an entrenched celebrity using the media to attack me." Knowing the court was about to see videotapes of the attacks, Vickie's lawyer struck out in desperation, accusing Marshall of hiring a public relations firm to "coddle the press."

In a 1995 videotape of the program *A Current Affair*, Anna Nicole Smith told the reporter that her husband's son, Pierce, had cut off her money and that she couldn't pay her bills. However, in Houston, the jurors were informed that Anna Nicole Smith had tens of thousands of dollars in her own bank accounts at the same time she claimed her utilities were being cut off. When asked why she needed an allowance of $5,000 a month, she responded, "It's expensive to be me…. It's terrible."

E. Pierce's team joked that on Planet Vickie, whatever ill befell her, "Pierce did it." Anna blamed E. Pierce for the fact that she had barely seen her husband during the period before he died. She said that he had hired private detectives to follow her around and guards to stop her from getting close to her husband.

Despite all of her attempts to film J. Howard, she never once caught him telling the camera that he would leave her half of his estate. He did say he wanted Anna to be looked after and perhaps that meant the same thing as leaving her half of his $1.6 billion wealth. However, it did not work in Anna's favor that even after they had got married, the will had been revised and still did not include her. On the other side, E. Pierce had been left in charge of the will up to the date it had been finalized and he therefore could have manipulated it to include whatever he wanted it to. He was the one dealing with the lawyers and therefore he could have asked them to write anything that left him the entire estate, even if it was not what J. Howard had intended.

BANKRUPT

*I*n May 1994, Anna's ex-nanny, Maria Cerrato, came forward and sued Anna Nicole for sexual assault and harassment. In her deposition, Anna said that she had been the victim and it was Maria who had come on to her. She said that for a few weeks Maria had been getting her drunk during the day and that, on more than one occasion, her friends had witnessed Maria taking her clothes off, then kissing and touching her while she was passed out. Anna realized that she was being taken advantage of and put an end to her drinking binge. Then, a couple of weeks later, Maria got into the bathtub with Anna while they were both sober and proposed to her.

One day while Anna was in Texas recovering from plastic surgery, Maria called her from L.A. completely drunk. It was 2 a.m. and she was meant to be babysitting Daniel. She wanted to go out and, when Anna screamed that she couldn't leave Daniel alone, Maria quit. Anna accepted her resignation, called Sam, her other babysitter, and told him to go to the house immediately.

When Sam got there he discovered that Maria had hired some people in a brown car and they were loading Anna's things into it. Maria attacked Sam when he tried to stop her from stealing

Anna's belongings and then she woke Daniel up and told him she was going to take him to Honduras with her.

Sam called the police and, when they arrived, Anna spoke to them over the phone. She told them her side of the story and that she wanted Maria out of her house. The brown car filled with Anna's stereo, jewelry, and God-knows-what else had already disappeared by the time the cops arrived, but they took back Anna's keys and barred Maria from returning.

Maria's side of the story is very different. She is Honduran and, when Anna first hired her, she could speak very little English. She treasured her job and was afraid of losing it. When Anna came on to her, she did not want to upset her employer by resisting. She allowed Anna to use her as a sex toy and kept quiet about it. Maria also claims that she was held captive by Anna in the house.

On August 18, 1995, Maria Antonia Cerrato won an $830,000 judgment against Anna Nicole Smith. Anna appealed the decision and lost.

Despite the hit to her bank balance, Anna managed to work the situation to her advantage. Losing that much money gave her the perfect opportunity to file for bankruptcy and liquidate her debts. In January 1996, while the Texas probate court case was still in progress, Anna decided that she was a resident of California and filed for Chapter 11 bankruptcy there.

Anna tried to portray herself as naive and uneducated. Yet, when she filed for bankruptcy in 1996, it was clear that she had had a small army of attorneys working for her for years. Her bankruptcy filings showed her owing approximately $350,000 to nine separate attorneys and law firms.

More significant is the fact that her listing of assets did not include any promise of continued financial support or half of everything her late husband owned. Asked how she could explain such a glaring omission of what would potentially be a major asset, Vickie told the court: "My lawyers deal with my cases, I don't."

"Can we assume that since you had not filed any document or told anybody by August 1995 that you hadn't told anybody about the promise?" asked Rusty Hardin.

"I don't remember," said Vickie. Pressed further on the issue, she again told Hardin, "I'll have to get with my lawyers."

Seeing through Anna's obvious ploy to avoid paying any of her debt, E. Pierce made sure that, even by declaring herself bankrupt, Anna would not be able to eliminate her debt to him. Usually the matter of J. Howard's inheritance would have been dealt with solely in the Texas probate court. But, on June 11, 1996, E. Pierce brought a counterclaim in Anna's bankruptcy case in California, alleging that Anna had defamed him by telling the press he had engaged in forgery, fraud, and overreaching to gain control of his father's assets. E. Pierce truly did make a federal case out of a local probate dispute.

On June 14, 1996, Vickie retaliated, asserting truth as a defense. She also filed a long list of incomprehensible counterclaims, which basically boiled down to the fact that E. Pierce had illegally interfered with her income and inheritance, and committed fraud in his dealings with J. Howard's trust and will.

Vickie's wrongful interference counterclaim turned her objection to Pierce's claim into an adversary proceeding. These claims were considered to fall under "core proceedings" which gave the bankruptcy court jurisdiction to dispose of the claims. The bankruptcy court held a five-day hearing, commencing on October 27, 1999. The court found that E. Pierce Marshall tortiously interfered with Vickie Lynn Marshall's expectancy that she would receive a so-called "*inter vivos*" gift (meaning an inheritance) from J. Howard Marshall II in the form of a catchall trust that would take effect upon his death. Marshall had set up a trust for Anna so that she would inherit half of his earnings during the time they were married.

On November 5, 1999, the bankruptcy court granted summary judgment for Anna on Pierce's complaint. It found that

Vickie had published no statements about Pierce, had not ratified any statements about Pierce made by her attorneys, and was not otherwise liable for any statements her attorneys had made about Pierce. Thus, the bankruptcy court decided that Vickie had not committed a willful or malicious act—the court cleared her of E. Pierce's accusations.

On October 6, 2000, the bankruptcy court awarded Anna compensatory damages in excess of $449 million, less whatever she recovered in the ongoing probate action in Texas—as well as $25 million in punitive damages. The court found that the younger Marshall had altered, destroyed and falsified documents to try to keep Anna from receiving money from his father's estate.

There was absolutely no way Pierce would let Anna get hold of any of his money and so he appealed to the United States District Court, which has the power to review decisions made in the bankruptcy court. The District Court decided that the bankruptcy court had exceeded its jurisdiction and reheard just about the entire case. The District Court ordered Pierce to produce over four hundred boxes of additional documents, making it one of the most extensive records ever produced in that court.

Anna's behavior in court was hilarious. The whole room was full of stiff-upper-lip men and then you had…Anna. She wore a suit for the occasion but nothing could have concealed the true Vickie. On the first day of the trial her attorneys asked the court to provide her a more comfortable chair because "she has a bad back." (In Houston, she used a minor accident with a barbell as an excuse to skip court and try to get out of the trial.) During the first week of her California trial, she was always late for court and frequently out of the courtroom. She also burst into tears at various times during the trial.

Anna Nicole Smith's performance in court was so bizarre that both attorney Rusty Hardin and Judge David O. Carter asked her if she was under the influence of any medication during her testimony. Anna seemed slightly dazed during much of her testimony and continually asked for simple questions to be repeated. She showed the same reluctance to answer specific questions that she had exhibited throughout this trial and the others before—even when she was being questioned by a federal judge.

Judge Carter: "I've seen you walk into court with a limp."

Vickie: "Can we talk about it in private?"

Judge Carter: "Have you been under medication?"

Vickie: "Can we please talk about it in private? I'm not on any medication at this time."

Maybe it's just coincidence, but part of Vickie's pattern seems to be to have a visible medical problem each time she came to court. Vickie made sure the courtroom shared her pain. In Houston, her attorney bandaged her injured hand in the courtroom, and Vickie held her bandaged hand up so that jurors couldn't miss it. In Santa Ana, Vickie appeared to walk with great difficulty. Yet, outside of the courtroom observers say her pain appeared to vanish.

Judge David O. Carter provided her with a more comfortable chair when he was told she had back problems. When asked about a specific medical condition, Vickie asked to be questioned about the subject "in private." Judge Carter may not have been aware medical experts testified in Houston that Vickie had exaggerated a minor injury. Even Vickie's own physician testified she was capable of coming to court.

Questioning Smith was like trying to pin Jell-O to the wall. Judge Carter acknowledged the problem when he told attorney Rusty Hardin, "I'm trying to give counsel leeway because of the way she answers questions."

Anna Nicole Smith did not explode on the stand or curse Hardin, as she did in Houston. According to the Orange County Register, Judge David O. Carter "shielded her from intense questioning by E. Pierce's attorney, Hardin. Numerous times the judge waved his hand downward to order Hardin to lower his voice."

Vickie's strategy as a witness was to claim she couldn't remember significant dates, to have even the simplest questions repeated over and over, or to answer a completely different question from the one that was asked.

The papers also noted that the court gave Hardin additional time to question Vickie because he "frequently had to ask questions numerous times before getting an answer from her."

The court stated early in this case that witnesses' credibility would be a major issue. Vickie began her testimony by stating under oath she was a Texas resident. Hardin showed numerous sworn statements she had signed saying she was a California resident. Vickie blamed the inconsistencies on her lawyers, saying, "I just sign where they put the sticky things."

Vickie avoided some of the issues that got her in trouble in Houston, where she accused Pierce Marshall of trying to have her killed. In California, she toned it down, saying only that she thought Pierce was capable of "doing her harm."

A lot of new information was revealed in the District Court review, especially in matters concerning E. Pierce's fraudulent activities and what J. Howard had really intended for Anna Nicole upon his death. Anna has always been an easy target to ridicule but her legal team did an outstanding job, turning the tables on her impenetrable opposition. Despite Anna's bizarre courtroom antics, her attorneys managed to bring down E. Pierce and the late J. Howard's clique.

In the fall of 1992, J. Howard directed his attorney, Harvey Sorensen, to draft a prenuptial agreement for him and his wife-to-be. This fifty-eight-page agreement was presented to him on November 18, 1992. According to the District Court, the prenuptial agreement provided that "upon the termination of the marriage by either death or divorce, Vickie was to receive $100,000 for each month that [they] were married. She would also get an additional $5 million if she and J. Howard had a child together. Largely as a result of J. Howard's lingering bitterness from Lady Walker's betrayal, J. Howard insisted that the draft agreement include a provision that if Vickie had intercourse with anyone other than J. Howard during their marriage, her payment would be reduced by half."

When the agreement was eventually drawn up, J. Howard thought that it was too long. He wanted something brief and to the point and so he went to his newly appointed attorney, Edwin Hunter, to revise it. Although the document was never finalized, it is clear that J. Howard wanted to leave Anna some form of inheritance. He confirmed this in a recorded message to the Texas probate judge on May 26, 1995, when he stated: "I want my wife to be supported by me."

J. Howard also wanted to give Anna gifts in other forms. He prepared a catchall trust for her, which would hold valuable assets until after he died. He also wanted to set up a company for her called the Marshall Farm Corporation. In much the same way as he had hired his mistress, Lady Walker, to be the director of his company, J. Howard also had Anna Nicole sign papers which would give his company the right to exploit her celebrity image in return for a salary. Do you really believe the conservative, billion-dollar oil syndicate would hire Anna Nicole Smith to represent it? I'm sure Koch's patriarchal board of directors was jumping with joy at the suggestion!

Another way J. Howard planned to avoid paying generation-skipping taxes was to *adopt* Vickie. However, luckily his attorney advised him that the Texas law might frown upon the type of relationship he was having with his new "daughter."

Lastly, J. Howard decided with his lawyer that he wanted to give Vickie half of his "new community" once they were married. This would mean she would inherit half of the increase in his assets during the time they were married. Vickie went one step further and, in court, testified that on at least two occasions J. Howard promised her "half of everything I have."

Anna's attorneys had a lot of ammunition in the argument against J. Howard's son and attorney, Edwin Hunter. Not only did they both have hidden motives for withholding information, Hunter also conspicuously denied knowing a lot of the events he had to have been involved in. In court, when Hunter was asked where the "catchall trust" was, he denied ever having heard of it. However, according to his billing records he had not only heard of it but, under J. Howard's instruction, helped create it. According to the records, he had telephoned his partner, Glazier, to discuss the catchall trust on December 16, 1994, and by December 21, 1994, Glazier had written the first draft.

With access to hundreds of thousands of pages of E. Pierce and Edwin Hunter's legal documents, the court was able to deduce that Hunter was working directly for E. Pierce behind J. Howard's back. They had nicknames for Anna such as "Miss Cleavage" and "Mischief," making it obvious that they didn't take her seriously. They schemed together to get rid of the problem posed in the form of a big-busted blonde. Hunter swore to the court that he was working directly in J. Howard's interest and that E. Pierce always followed his father's orders. However, by comparing the four hundred seventy boxes of paperwork, the court discovered that some of the documents were backdated after they had been delivered. Hunter had researched annulling the marriage before it had even taken place, and on July 8, 1994, he faxed a plan to E. Pierce, detailing what Anna would get after they were married, which he never showed to J. Howard.

Just to prove what a liar he was, Hunter made financial decisions that would have been beneficial to J. Howard had he lived for five more years. At ninety years old, J. Howard's health was in a severe crisis. He was deemed to be so senile that he had to sign over a power of attorney; his heart had stopped on more than one occasion, and he was considered by his doctor to be "close to death." He was committed to twenty-four-hour nursing care and his lawyer had begun looking into funeral arrangements. If this wasn't enough for Hunter to realize that J. Howard would not live for five more years, in spring 1995, J. Howard's physician, Dr. Reed, diagnosed him with terminable and inoperable stomach cancer. He informed Hunter that J. Howard had as little as three months to live.

Nevertheless, Hunter insists that J. Howard agreed to give up his last assets in exchange for a profit that he would never see. J. Howard would have to have been suffering from senile dementia to sign away his money for five years when he was probably going to die in three months.

When the Living Trust was finalized in July 1994, J. Howard and Pierce were its co-trustees. In writing, Hunter expressed his concerns over who should take over as J. Howard's successor upon his death and suggested: "The longest serving federal judge in Texas." Guess who the longest serving federal judge in Texas was at that time? Edwin Hunter's father, the Honorable Edwin F. Hunter, Jr., Senior District Judge for the Western District of Louisiana. Perfect! If Edwin Hunter could not get his hands on J. Howard's inheritance, at least his father would be able to.

By the time J. Howard died, none of his life-long and trusted attorneys wanted anything to do with Edwin Hunter. They would not support his decisions because they could see through what they understood to be his manipulative and deceptive tactics. They believed he was self-motivated and corrupt and conspired with his employer's son to make a fortune for himself.

E. Pierce was not oblivious to the goings on and also had his own agenda.

He would rather have spent every last penny of his father's wealth, than see his wicked stepmother get any of it. He had already seen the repercussions of J. Howard's extravagant gifts to his last mistress, Lady Diane Walker, and he was not going to let it happen again.

It was E. Pierce who had hired Edwin Hunter to take over the estate plan and his father had backed up his choice. It is clear from the records that as soon as Hunter was put in charge, he made drastic changes to the estate plan. He knew J. Howard did not have long to live and so he worked fast.

Even though J. Howard preferred one- or two-page documents, Hunter drew up hundreds of pages of detailed records. J. Howard also had cataracts in his eyes and so could not read unless the writing was huge and, even then, only with glasses. He often asked E. Pierce and Hunter to read the documents to him, making it easy for them to distort or completely delete entire sections. The Old Man merely signed on the dotted line when he was told to.

E. Pierce claims that he did not know about the wedding until weeks after it had happened. This seems to be a blatant lie since there are records to show that Hunter had informed him about it, even prior to the wedding. The day after the ceremony, E. Pierce and Hunter had a meeting with one of J. Howard's business associates, Henry Schlesinger, who had been invited to the wedding. There is no doubt that J. Howard's son knew about the wedding before or, if not, immediately after it had taken place.

Pierce had kept quiet since the beginning of their legal battle but in 2001 he finally spoke out: "Anna Nicole Smith could not show anything that I did to prevent her from receiving expectancy. Anna Nicole Smith could not show that I knew anything about expectancy. How could I interfere with a gift I knew nothing about?

"It was her word vs. the live testimony of three respected attorneys who represented my father for 13 years and more than 2 million pages of supporting documents. What influence other than the facts and the law are at work here?"

Pierce knew how to work the media to his advantage. Only his tactics were much more subtle and conniving than Anna's. He obviously did not want people to know that he had been aware of the wedding because, within two weeks, he and Hunter had changed J. Howard's entire estate plan to stop Anna from getting anything. As soon as Pierce found out that his father was planning to marry Anna and make a substantial gift to her, he went about draining his father of all of his assets. Hunter made it impossible for J. Howard to take out any money from his oil company, therefore preventing him from giving Anna any gifts. According to Anna's lawyers, Hunter and Pierce made sure that the trust could not be reversed once it was finalized. They then backdated the documents so that it looked like they had been drawn up and signed before the wedding had taken place.

Prior to the documents being completed, they also had J. Howard and Anna followed by secret detectives in order to make sure that J. Howard would not draft up a new will behind his son's back. Even if he did manage to sign anything over to Vickie without them knowing, they had a backup plan. By backdating the documents it would void any gift that J. Howard might have intended Anna to have.

After the trust was signed by J. Howard, an extra page was added making it irreversible. J. Howard had no idea that he had been stripped of almost all of his money and that there was nothing he could do about it. Even a year later, J. Howard believed he had total control over his assets. His attorney, Glenn Johnson, is quoted as saying, "He trusted Pierce and had no problem with it [his estate plan], and if he ever didn't like it, he could change it." Apparently he couldn't!

The Living Trust was not the only document E. Pierce and Edwin Hunter destroyed, backdated, altered and lied about. With the help of a forensic expert, additional records, and witnesses, the pair's scheming ways were exposed by the District Court's new trial.

Edwin Hunter publicly denied the finding of Anna's legal team: "E. Pierce's inheritance of the family business remained unchanged since 1982 as recorded in a carefully documented series of six wills and seven trusts." E. Pierce's defense attorney, Rusty Hardin, stated he showed the court that Anna Nicole Smith's attorneys had received other materials they claimed were withheld. They had chosen not to use the documents because they would lower the wildly inflated value Anna Nicole Smith's legal team had tried to place on the estate.

Like a child digging through a pile of manure hoping to find a pony, Vickie's attorneys had based their case on continually escalating demands for discovery of all documents referring to J. Howard's estate. But after more than four hundred seventy-five boxes containing over two million pages of documents had been produced, including material that should be covered by attorney-client privilege, Vickie's attorneys still didn't have their smoking gun. Nor had they found any other evidence to show J. Howard planned to give her more than the $6.7 million he had provided during his lifetime.

Pierce Marshall reminded Vickie's attorney that his father was an attorney who, when he agreed to something orally, always put it in writing. "If dad was serious about it, he always backed it up in writing. He was a lawyer. He knew the importance of written documents." Marshall said, "Dad never told me about any commitment to Vickie. No one has ever come forward [with evidence of an oral agreement] in thirteen lawsuits."

Despite spending hundreds and thousands of dollars on legal bills, again E. Pierce was found guilty of interfering with Vickie's expectancy; for conspiring to suppress or destroy the *inter vivos* gift; and to strip J. Howard of his assets by backdating, altering, and otherwise falsifying documents and presenting them to J. Howard under false pretenses.

On a final note, the court took into consideration what J. Howard had actually intended Vickie to have. There was a lot of evidence to show that he wanted her to have half of everything he owned but this could not be proved. What is more, Vickie went on

Howard Stern's radio show two days before J. Howard died and publicly announced that she was not expecting to get anything from J. Howard's will. Anna testified that the reason she had said this was as part of a publicity campaign. She did not want people to think that she had married J. Howard only for his money.

Her lawyer contradicted this in his closing statement, arguing that she *only* married him for financial security. "What is he offering?" her attorney asked. "Does this court really believe a man reputed to be the richest man in Texas offered her his good looks, longevity, fatherhood?"

Even if nobody but Anna knew whether or not he had promised her half of everything, what can be proved is that J. Howard did intend to give Anna half of his "new community." He wanted her to have one-half of the growth of his assets during the time of the marriage. The supporting evidence lies in statements that he made to various witnesses, as well as instructions he gave to his lawyers when he was discussing potential prenuptial agreements.

The court set about re-evaluating what half of J. Howard's "new community" would have added up to, had it not been interfered with by E. Pierce and Edwin Hunter, and awarded Anna compensatory damages in the sum of $44,292,767.33, plus her legal expenses. A lot less than what Anna had previously been awarded but, all the same, a hell of a lot of money. The court also compensated Vickie for the harm that had been inflicted on her by E. Pierce. It decided that E. Pierce's actions were a lot more malicious than the bankruptcy court had thought and calculated the punitive damages to be $44,292,767.33, making a total of $88,585,534.66.

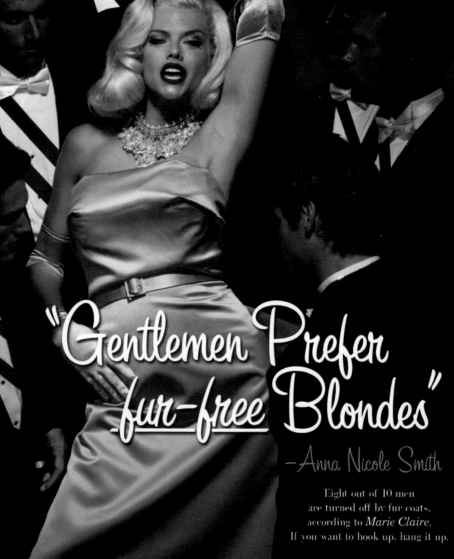

"*Gentlemen Prefer fur-free Blondes*"

—Anna Nicole Smith

Eight out of 10 men
are turned off by fur coats,
according to *Marie Claire*.
If you want to hook up, hang it up.

Photo: Robert Sebree

Photograph © Robert Sebree

Anna poses as Marilyn Monroe for a 2004 PETA ad campaign entitled, "Gentlemen Prefer Fur Free Blondes."

Left to right: Ginger Mitchell, Linda Compton and Vickie Hogan (before she became Anna Nicole)
in front of 6th grade teacher, Mr. Yawn.

Vickie Lynn Smith's driver license in 1994 before she changed her name.

Vickie Lynn Smith's ID card in 1994.

Sandi Powledge, Anna's lesbian lover, and Anna show off their tattoos with Daniel in 1993.

Left: Cousin Brandy with Anna's half sisters, Donna and Amy.

A special note from Anna to her baby sister Donna.

Donnie Hogan with his sister, Anna, in the back of a limo on the way back from a party.
Donnie carried this photo in his wallet for 15 years.

Family photo of Anna with her mother, Virgie; her first husband, Billy Smith;
and their 2-month-old son, Daniel.

Anna with her son Daniel and attorney Howard K. Stern in 2002.

Anna aged 26 and J. Howard Marshall II aged 89 on their wedding day, June 27, 1994.

This photo of Anna, wrapped in faux fur, was taken by her former boyfriend, Larry Birkhead at comedian Eddie Murphy's former mansion in Los Angeles. It was to promote the relaunch of her website that was to take place on April 7, 2005.

Anna kissing her late son Daniel's cheek at "G-Phoria, The Award Show for Gamers," which was held at the Shrine Expo Center in Los Angeles, July 31, 2004.

Donna's mother Wanda with children (top to bottom) Donna, Donnie and Amy.

Donna (left), Amy and Donnie at Christmas 1979.

Christmas at Grandma Lucille's house, where Donna mostly grew up. Left to right: Donna's cousin, Carrie; Donnie; cousin Wendy holding her baby sister, Shari; Donna and cousin Cindy.

Donna Hogan in 2nd grade.

Donnie and Amy Hogan.

ANNA DONNA

Kodak

Sisters, Anna and Donna at Anna's calendar signing in 1994.

Wanda and Donnie on the first day Amy was brought home from hospital.

Anna's half-sister Amy with their father, Donald Hogan.

Donald Hogan and Aunt Linda.

Left to right: Anna's nieces and nephews: Andrew, Brandon, Timmy, Ashley and Kayla.

Back right: Donna's son Brandon in his soccer team photo.

Ashley and Kayla in the front middle of the cheerleading squad. Donna's friend April is in the back middle.

Donna with her friend April's daughter, Rebecca.

Amy's daughter Alexis.

Left to right: Brandon, Donna, Kayla, April, with her daughter Becky, and Ashley at Key West, Florida.

Anna and Donna's brother Donnie with his twin boys, Donnie Ray and Danny Ray Hogan, on their first day of school.

Donna's younger brother, Larry Hogan.

Maurizio, the Greek hotel tycoon.

Left to right: Ashley, Brandon and Kayla at Halloween, 2000.

Donnie Hogan at Anna's Playmate of the Year Party at the Playboy Mansion, 1993.

Barbara Moore and Donnie Hogan at Hugh Hefner's Playboy Mansion, 1993.

Donna and April in Texas, 2005.

Donnie's wife, Mickie.

Anna's dad, Donald Hogan, Vince Neil from Motley Crue and Anna's brother Donnie at Vince's house.

For the Love of Dogs, Boycott Iams.

—ANNA NICOLE SMITH

Marilyn, Sugar Pie, and Puppy ARE BOYCOTTING IAMS UNTIL IT STOPS TESTING ON ANIMALS IN LABS.

Visit IamsCruelty.com FOR MORE DETAILS

PeTA

Anna poses for a 2005 PETA ad campaign against the Iams dog food company's tests on dogs.

DOWNHILL CAREER

"Celebrity is a mask that eats into the face.
As soon as one is aware of being somebody,
to be watched and listened to with extra
interest, input ceases, and the performer
goes blind and deaf in his over animation.
One can either see or be seen."
—JOHN UPDIKE

While the legal battles continued, the talent-deprived Anna Nicole Smith still managed to keep a Hollywood career alive, with projects that included *Anna Nicole Smith: Exposed*, a show on which she took co-writer, co-director, and associate producer credits.

Her director friend, Ray Martino, cast her in his porn movie. He is the same friend with whom she visited J. Howard when she was thrown out of the hospital at two in the morning. He is also the same man with whom she overdosed on "painkillers" just before she ended up at the Betty Ford Clinic in November 1995.

They wrote the script together, basing the story line on a day in the life of Anna Nicole. They must have really taxed themselves writing the plot, which is centered on nothing other than

Anna Nicole taking her clothes off and leading us through her daily masturbation techniques. Landing herself the ideal role, she didn't even need to act; she just played herself.

The only time I watched clips of the movie was accidentally, as it was interspersed with some other footage. Funnily enough, her exposé got a better rating than most of her later film choices. Showing off her body while it was still svelte, she succeeded in winning over a lot of horny men. However, when she kept her clothes on, she did not have as much luck with her critics.

She dropped from three out of ten stars to a mere two when she played another one of Ray Martino's leading ladies. In *Skyscraper*, Anna was cast as a seductive action hero. Unfortunately, she could not save her enemy's hostages with the same conviction as Arnold Schwartzenegger and the movie went straight to video.

She was given guest appearances in *Ally McBeal* and *Veronica's Closet* and her career trajectory seemed to be improving when she was cast as a doctor in a new television series, *N.Y.U.K.*, but the show quickly folded.

Anna's failing career and reputation did not make my life as her sister any easier. The locals tormented me nearly all the time, especially when the newspapers decided to document her latest shenanigans.

Around the time Anna's direct-to-video porn movie came out in the stores, I heard rumors that one of the local policewomen, Officer "Alice" (not her real name), wanted to arrest me. A few years earlier, my long-term ex-boyfriend, "Jerry" (also not his real name), had trained her to be a police officer and so we had known each other for a while. She went on to become Jerry's work partner and so we spent a lot of time around each other. I got the feeling that she didn't like me from the beginning. As a woman, she saw me as competition and was always hostile towards me.

After Jerry and I split up, Alice stopped working with him but our paths crossed again when I started dating her ex. Even though she was married and he was her boss, I heard that Alice and the chief of police had had a two-month-long affair. Just after she apparently split up with him, the police chief and I started dating for a short period of time and that is when she really had it in for me. On top of that, Alice really liked another guy whom I later dated, fuelling her competitive envy even more.

Alice was rumored to be bragging to all her friends and the other officers that she was going to arrest Anna Nicole Smith's sister. She apparently said that she was going to make my life miserable when I was sent to jail by telling all my cellmates that I was Anna's sister so they would all hate me.

One week later, I was sitting in a restaurant with some friends of mine and Alice walked in and sat at a nearby table. I immediately knew something was up because the waitress there was a friend of hers and started giving us a really hard time. My friend and the waitress got into an argument because she wouldn't give my friend her card back and we wanted to leave. I knew I had to get out of there and didn't want to cause any trouble so I tried to intervene and tell them to drop it. Alice jumped at the opportunity and arrested me for drunk and disorderly behavior, even though I was stone cold sober and hadn't done anything wrong. Just to add the icing on the cake, the manager of the restaurant, who was Alice's best friend, put on a police jacket and offered support. They both accused us of stirring up trouble when we quite obviously hadn't done anything and the whole series of events was caught on camera.

I couldn't believe what was happening, but I didn't want to make an even bigger fuss by defending myself. I knew that this was too ridiculous for them to get away with and so I let them arrest me. The officers also did a security check on my friend, who unfortunately had a warrant at the time, and so they took us both to the local police station and put us in jail for the night.

I later learned that Officer Alice wasn't even within her work vicinity at the time of the arrest. I was told that she was supposed to be on duty somewhere else. It seems to me that it should be a crime to arrest me for no reason, outside of her patrol area. It took months of investigation and trials for the truth to come out and, when it did, the chief of police begged me to drop the charges. That's the same police chief I had had an affair with and whom Alice had initially been so jealous of. I was told that he had known way in advance that Alice had planned to arrest me for no reason, but he had done nothing to stop it. I didn't see why I should put myself on the line when he hadn't even prevented me from getting arrested in the first place so I had no reservations going ahead with the charges.

The restaurant manager got charged with impersonating a police officer, and the chief of police and Alice got fired. A whole bunch of other police officers in that precinct got laid off too. It wasn't just because of me; an investigation concluded they had been committing all sorts of crimes.

Alice left the city where she was working and moved to another county. She got hired as a police officer there, but the next I heard of her was on the news. She made the headlines for alleged sexual activity with an inmate and according to the story, was barred from ever being an officer again. This just confirmed my opinion that the only thing on Alice's mind was where her next lay was coming from, whether it was her husband, her boss, the chief of police, or an inmate. I never did hear what happened to Alice or the outcome of the charges.

At around the same time, Anna was being harassed by her one-time boyfriend, Mark Hatten, who began stalking her. Anna claimed that she had a brief sexual fling with him in 2000, but ended their relationship when he threatened her with a knife. She took him to court, with allegations of assault with a deadly weapon and battery. He had beaten up Anna's neighbor, Rene Navarro, for trying to stop a fight between him and Anna. Navarro ended up needing surgery on his hand because of the damage done during the attack.

Despite the evidence against him, Hatten tried to convince the court to let him go free by saying: "I'm not a bad person, I'm an excellent candidate for probation.... If I have to go to prison, it's your call. [But] you'll never hear about me bothering Anna Nicole again or [her neighbor]."

I mean come on! Did he really believe the judge would fall for his promises? He had a record of previous violence (no surprises there with our family's track record of abusive men); he had harassed Anna with a barrage of phone calls and threatened to come to her house with a gun; he had held a knife to her in her own house; and he wouldn't leave her alone when she asked him to. This left Anna no choice but to take him to court, and then when he got there Hatten swore to the judge he would never bother his ex-lover again. Anyway, Judge Kathryn Stoltz didn't fall for his pathetic promises and in November he was convicted on two of the four charges. Due to his violent history, the judge nearly put him away for the maximum penalty charge of nine years. Instead, he got away with six years and eight months.

After Anna died and the story came out about J. Howard Marshall's sperm being frozen, Mark sent *TMZ.com* and *Extra* a letter saying that he had also had his sperm frozen for Anna and that he could possibly be Dannielynn's father. After being convicted for stalking Anna, it is highly unlikely that she would want him to father her child. It seems to me that the letter, sent from Pleasant Valley State Prison, was nothing but a desperate attempt for his fifteen minutes of fame. He is obsessed with her, has tattoos of her across his entire back, and has spent time behind bars drawing her portrait over and over again.

Furthermore, his sister Jackie Hatten appeared on *Larry King Live*, telling the world that she was Anna's best friend and that her brother had had a long-term relationship with Anna. What she failed to mention was that their love affair had turned sour and her brother was still in prison, serving his sentence.

CHAPTER 14

PUBLICIST

*A*nna always had an entourage. From the time she sent in her photos to *Playboy*, Anna had a support team, including agents, publicists, friends, family, and lawyers. However, once Howard K. Stern came into the picture, he took over all the roles, and everyone else was dropped.

David Granoff was Anna's publicist from the beginning. Back when she was an elite model and Playmate of the Year, Anna had sought him out. She had read about his A-list clientele and refused to have anyone but him represent her. She called David directly, took him to lunch, and wrote a check on the spot. That was the beginning of a relationship that would last for eleven years.

David said that Anna made his job easy. "Every story would be old news by the time it came out. She made a name for herself out of nothing and with her looks she could have conquered the world."

One day when Anna was representing Guess? on tour, she called David from Japan. She was afraid for her life. Everyone there had dark hair and, whether or not they knew who she was, they would grab at her platinum-blonde locks. Anna looked different from everyone else and the crowds would stare at her and try to touch her skin as if she were a tourist attraction. Anna was scared and she called David to tell him what was going on. He immediately turned it into a huge story, which made the "People" page in *Time* magazine the following week. David made sure they also included a risqué photo of Anna, even though it went against their policy.

As we all know, Anna's public life was very transient. If you ever got bored of her antics, you just had to wait a day or two for a complete turnaround. However, Anna didn't need a publicist to invent stories for the media; her private life was equally turbulent. People were always coming and going in Anna's world. One day it was her father and brother, the next it was her mother, aunt and uncle, cousins, string of men, or even me. There was always a flavor of the month, which then turned sour and disappeared off the face of the earth.

David Granoff said it was always fun working for Anna, especially in the beginning. He believed she should have gone a lot further than she did. She had the right looks and a larger-than-life personality to go with it, but she did not surround herself with the right people. Most of the men she dated used her and dragged her down with them. If they did not steal from her, they misplaced her things accidentally in a delirious state, but either way they were up to no good. A lot of the people Anna surrounded herself with took drugs and were a bad influence on her. Maybe that explains why her life was always full of drama and tragedy.

When Anna hired David in 1993, he did not charge her, but she reassured him, "Don't worry, I'll take care of you." David was in charge of all of Anna's PR for the first couple of years of her career. During that period, her career skyrocketed. Then she added an extra dimension to her management team: a string of agents, who caused a lot of conflict between David and Anna and put an end to their partnership.

Their differences were eventually resolved with the help of a high-powered entertainment attorney, Robert Hantman. Although they became friends again, David stopped representing

Anna and she fell out of sight. After J. Howard died, Anna sank into depression. She indulged in drugs and put on a lot of weight.

It was not until 1998, that Anna got back into shape and approached David to work for her again. She told him, "David, I want to get back into things. Will you represent me?" He sympathized with her, saying, "I like the underdog. My name is David; like David and Goliath." He willingly obliged and helped revive Anna's career and celebrity image.

The entire time David worked for Anna, she did not pay him. He had worked on and off for her for eleven years on the basis that she would "take care of him" once she saw any money herself. When she got her reality show, the original pitch came through David. He realized that in order to make his work for her legitimate, he needed Anna to sign a document to confirm her promise that, when she got paid, she would pay him.

David wrote to Anna to ask her for something in writing. He included how much she owed him—a smallish amount—and asked her to confirm that she would eventually pay it when she could afford to. Howard K. Stern was already in the picture by then and decided to take the matter into his own hands. He wrote back to David telling him he had spoken to Anna who said that David was never her publicist and, therefore, they did not owe him anything.

The whole world knew that David Granoff had been acting as Anna's publicist. He was the one anyone called if they needed to get to her. He even had paparazzi shots taken alongside Anna through the years, captioned as being her publicist.

David was forced to seek the advice of an attorney and went to one of the best: Benedict Morelli. Morelli agreed to represent David and they sued Anna *and* Howard in two separate lawsuits. They both settled and David finally saw some of the money he had been owed for a decade.

After the case was over, Anna called David up and asked him, "Why are you doing this?" She had no idea what had been going on, which makes me wonder if Howard K. Stern actually discussed the matter with her in the first place. It further leads me to question if any other decisions were made on Anna's behalf without her ever knowing.

CHAPTER 15

THE ANNA NICOLE SHOW

"It's not supposed to be funny....
It just is."

—E! ENTERTAINMENT
PROMO LINE

When MTV debuted the wildly popular reality series, *The Osbournes* in 2002, E! wasted no time following suit. The network had already dedicated an episode of *True Hollywood Story* to Anna Nicole in 1997 and had received an unexpected response from audiences; her story quickly became the series' highest-rated episode. As she had already proved that she could pull in their target audience, the entertainment channel decided that a reality series about Anna Nicole Smith would be a good investment.

Anna Nicole was to star in her own television show, a non-fiction format, in which the cameras followed her around as she lived her day-to-day life. The crew would film her as she looked at houses to rent, worked with a fru-fru gay decorator, Bobby Trendy, stuffed her face with food and alcohol, fussed over her son Daniel, and so on. She could not even get through the first episode, without mock whispering to the camera that she really wanted to get home to get herself off. "That's the real fun," she says. "I didn't get to masturbate this morning; now it's time to go home."

"Dreadful" is far too complimentary a term to describe the series, which lasted for about a year. The theme tune to the show says it all with its lyrics:

Anna Anna Glamorous Anna, Anna Nicole

Born in Texas, strugglin', savin', trying to get some fame

Used what you got and that was a lot

You became a household name.

You married a billionaire, so he was 88, you didn't care

It all disappeared as fast as it came!

Anna Anna glamorous Anna, Anna Nicole

Anna Anna fabulous Anna, Anna Nicole

You're so outrageous: Anna Nicole.

In one of the episode specials, Anna gives a commentary. While the opening credits are playing she explains that it is all intended to shove her success in the faces of everyone she left behind in Mexia. There is a picture of Jim's Krispy Fried Chicken restaurant where she first worked. She laughs and says that's funny. She says she loved her employers, Jim and Joanna, even though they hated her.

Next there is a cartoon of Anna bouncing off a scale with wads of money and she says that it is meant as a big "fuck you" to everybody. She hesitates, saying that she has mixed feelings about all this; maybe it's not the right way to treat the people who were once her only friends and family. However, self-doubt was not one of Anna's fortes and you can see that the idea was forgotten the moment it left her pouting lips.

What is hilarious is that *The Anna Nicole Show* was supposed to be reality TV, but there was nothing truthful or spontaneous about it. Jay Leno was quick to notice this, joking, "They call it a reality show. See, that's what I love about L.A. It's the only place where a woman with bleached blonde hair, collagen lips, and fake boobs is considered reality. That's reality."

Her body was not the only thing in the show that was fake. Anna used the camera crew to show the world what she wanted them to see. On the show, once she has moved into her new house, the first thing Anna does is decide where to display her late husband's ashes. She carries the urn around with her, cherishing it as if it contained gold dust, until she eventually chooses to exhibit J. Howard's remains on top of the TV set. Anna is teary eyed, reminiscing over the good times when J. Howard was alive. She tells us that she misses him and that these ashes are her most prized possession. What she somehow forgets to mention is the fact that she had left her share of the ashes on the funeral home shelf for five years, until she realized that to abandon them entirely would not bode well in her court battle for the Old Man's will.

She had also done a special on *Entertainment Tonight* in which she spread J. Howard's ashes around her home. When someone is cremated, you only get so many ashes; how much of them could have been left in the urn after they were scattered around her entire ranch? For all we know she could have been crying over some recently dug-up soil.

Throughout the show, Anna somehow manages to be even less coherent than Ozzy Ozbourne and she is quite obviously on an assortment of drugs and alcohol. Even when she is sober, her lack of education smacks you in the face, but it is almost as if she is trying to appear stupid. She admits that she never reads because she hates it, and when she does try to read a sex scene from a Henry Miller book, Howard K. Stern has to pronounce the words for her. On another occasion Stern tells her to campaign in favor of Jews. Her response is a completely vacant look. To fill in for her, Kimmie says, "I think she'll stay neutral on this one," and Anna agrees saying, "I know nothing about nothing. Oh yes! Oh yes!"

Her weight problem did her no favors in front of the camera, which is known for adding extra pounds anyway. Nothing can deter her from eating; she is filmed with something in her mouth all day long. She even goes to the extreme of forcing everyone to have an eating competition with her. She orders round after round of heavy pizza and pasta dishes until she is sweating and has to run to the bathroom to throw up the food so that she can eat more.

When Anna gets back to the table Howard K. Stern accuses her of throwing up. She has a fit, shouting at him and insisting that she did not and that she can't believe he would think such a thing. She then storms out of the restaurant and refuses to speak to Howard because his accusations were so insulting. What she doesn't realize is that the cameras recorded her throwing up on national TV and Howard K. Stern had been standing outside the bathroom while she did it. The only thing Anna's adamant denial proves is that she can lie and to what lengths she will go to back herself up.

At the very beginning of the show she says that there are claims that she is fat, but really it is her big bones that make her look overweight. As if wanting to accentuate her "big bones," Anna insists on wearing skimpy clothes in which all her excess bulges are squirming to get out. She repeatedly gets stuck in the bathtub, in between chair legs, and any other tight spot she tries to squeeze into, and most of the time she has to be held or lifted in order to hoist herself up. She always tells the camera that she has to lose some weight but she never makes an attempt to do so. Instead she eats so much junk food that her dentist told her she needed twenty crowns. I mean TWENTY crowns are a lot, by anyone's standards. Hell, even George Washington had less dental work done in the 1700s. She claims that she grinds her teeth down to the nerves due to stress but, if anything, drugs make you grind your teeth and all the sugar she eats is what is causing them to crumble away.

Speaking of teeth, out of all of Anna's respectable relatives, she decided to introduce her toothless cousin to her 4.1 million viewers. Michelle Cloud a.k.a. Shelly is first spotted on the show while spying on Anna with another film crew. A company that is producing an unauthorized documentary of Anna has paid for Shelly's ticket to Los Angeles, but Anna refuses to see her. Howard K. Stern is forced to give her the bad news and Shelly breaks down crying, saying that she doesn't care about the documentary; she just misses her cousin and desperately wants to see her.

Shelly slides some photos of her sick baby in an incubator through the mail slot to Anna and, sympathetically, Anna eventually agrees to see her on the condition that the documentary crew not be there. They go for dinner and the entire time Anna could not look more uncomfortable. Shelly accepts one drink after another but refuses any food; she talks incessantly and asks Anna for money at least three times during their one meal together. Anna tells the camera that she has already paid for Shelly to have her black teeth whitened but that Shelly obviously didn't look after them as they have all fallen out. What neither of them mention is that Shelly is a drug addict and a terrible mother. She has five children but doesn't have custody of any of them. The worst thing about Anna parading this white trash relative of hers to the world is that everyone thinks it's me! Not all her relatives are like Shelly and it is truly upsetting that she was the one representing our family on Anna's show.

During the Christmas special, Shelly again shows up uninvited. She gets completely smashed and, on the commentary, Anna says that she was asking men to go home with her, despite being married. We see Shelly screeching on a microphone at the top of her lungs, deafening everyone around her. She is trying to sing karaoke but it sounds like an amplified drowning cat and everyone around her looks too embarrassed to say anything.

Anna's muscular bodybuilder friend goes topless and Shelly follows suit, flashing her pale, braless chest to the entire party as well as the millions of viewers. When this does not get her enough attention, she goes outside and jumps into the Jacuzzi, fully clothed in a white, soon to be see-through, suit. Howard K. Stern finds her and is forced to pull her out, fearing that he will be faced with a death suit if he leaves her there to drown. Having attracted this one-man audience, she puts on another show and starts to strip for the lawyer.

While Anna and her friends are drunk and mellow, singing carols and reading stories, Shelly feels inclined to lift up her top yet again and starts screaming at everyone. When she is escorted to bed she starts shouting even louder and attacks two of Anna's female friends. She hits them and manages to push one of them onto the floor. She refuses to go to bed and continues to act up so she can to get her fifteen minutes of fame. Shelly is a perfect example of Anna's family using her for both money and public attention. However, not all of us are like that.

I have always tried to give my relatives' names and numbers to the media so that they could get the publicity rather than me, but somehow they always come back for my story. Anna criticizes me for selling out on her and tells the media horrible things about me, but I have always been there for Anna when she needed me. I have never begged her for money, I do not take drugs, and I am a good mother.

During the entire two seasons, *The Anna Nicole Show* managed to evade her active sex life. Although she talks about sex incessantly: she goes to porn shops, strip bars, sex shows and humps anything around her, we never actually see her having sex or even alluding to it. In fact Anna claims that she has not had sex for two years when we all know that this is a downright lie.

When asked why she has not had a man for so long she says she cannot trust anybody. "I get sued all the time. I can't trust anybody. I mean, people I don't even know sue me all the time. I just don't trust anybody. It's hard." She has never been able to trust men in the past either and it has not stopped her before. She says she is forced to stay at home and can never go out and meet people, yet she is filmed partying on her show all the time.

In order to find a man she can trust, she joins a millionaire dating service. To qualify you have to have $1 million in your bank account and you have to pay a yearly $20,000 bill. Anna has a meeting with the matchmaker, Patti Stranger, who asks her what she sees in a man. Anna tells her that she likes men that are big and bear-like; that is pretty much her only specification. Her first date is with Claude Dauman, an Internet tycoon, who looks anything but muscular. Sticking to her chastity story, she says that she hasn't been on a date or with any man for two years. Well, that is if you don't count the guy that she admits to screwing for three weeks!

Claude goes all out and takes her to a fancy Japanese restaurant. They use the VIP elevator and have the whole dining room to themselves. The chef is there just for them and he cooks the food at their table. They are served the most expensive meat you can buy: Wagyu beef. It comes from cows that are cultivated in Japan. The cattle there are treated better than most people and the story is that they are fed beer and get massaged daily so that their flesh is exceptionally tender. It is known as the caviar of beef as the record price for one carcass is $250,000; the average is a mere $10,000-$20,000! None of this seems to impress Anna though, and she requests A1 sauce to go with her meal. This is obviously unheard of and one of the staff members has to be sent to the local store to buy it for her.

As soon as they are finished, she suggests they go to The Saddle Ranch, on the Sunset Strip, for bull riding. Having just eaten the rarest beef in the world, she orders herself a huge steak and devours the entire plate. She is clearly not at all attracted to her date, even telling the camera that she will have to drink like a fish to get through an evening with him. She definitely sticks to her word and passes out on his lap on the way home, probably intentionally so that he cannot make a pass at her. It is all very contrived and uncomfortable; they clearly have nothing to say to each other. He asks her who her favorite artist is and she replies: Marilyn Monroe. He gives her a lecture about how beauty is from within and she reciprocates with an uncomfortable silence. He waits for a few seconds and then tells her that he loves silence, even though he doesn't stop talking throughout the entire meal. It is all very weird to me.

Perhaps it is the gradual realization that this "reality" program is in fact staged, that led to the show's fall in ratings. The producers were telling Anna exactly what to do in order to generate enough scandal around the show when there was definitely no need to coerce Anna into playing up even more for her audience. Between them, "reality" had no role to play in the charade. Maybe it was this or maybe the viewers could no longer bear to watch her incomprehensible mumbling, unpleasant behavior and vast weight gain. In any case, for whatever reason, the viewers turned off and the show was cancelled in February 2004, with the official reason cited as "irreconcilable differences."

CHAPTER 16

TRIMSPA BABY

*"We asked her to re-create the famous
Marilyn Monroe pose for the
centerfold of our Icon issue....
I was there and can 100 per cent
vouch that she had no scars."*

—ROGER PADILHA AT
FASHION WEEK MAGAZINE

nna insisted that during the recording of her reality series the camera never once left her side. She went so far as to say they continued to film her in between seasons so that they wouldn't miss a beat. And yet somehow she managed to lose almost a hundred pounds—more than a baby in weight—without the camera capturing this miracle.

She had finally had enough of all the fat jokes at her expense. On *The Tonight Show*, Jay Leno asked, "How many watched Anna Nicole Smith? Did you see that? You see that thing on the E Channel? I think the E stands for enormous. Oh my god. Should have put that thing on the Food Channel. Stop it."

In 2003, Anna acted in a low-budget movie called *Wasabi Tuna*, in which she was the only one to play herself. The entire plot is based around kidnapping her dog, Sugar Pie, and making fun of Anna Nicole. It is a spoof on her life and there are five drag queens who dress up to look like her at the end of the movie. One of them is a midget. Another, Alexis Arquette, says that Anna never saw the funny side of the script, even though it was only written in order to dish on her.

Alexis was done up to look like an even more trashy version of Anna, with makeup streaming down her face. Anna was insulted that she might be perceived as a mess. She did not like the way she looked in the movie, stuffed into tight clothes and complained non-stop on the set, making everyone's life a misery.

Anna appeared briefly in the movie. In the main scene she stars in, her toe gets stuck in the faucet and, in mock pain, Anna calls for Kimmie, the assistant from her reality show. Her other appearance is in Mr. Ing's Chinese restaurant with Howard K. Stern and Kimmie, where, not surprisingly, she is eating again. This is a spoof of *The Anna Nicole Show*, as the waiter pointedly mentions "no eating contest."

As well as her dog, Anna's urn has been kidnapped. Apparently the enemy put drugs in it and, when Anna recognizes the urn in their possession, she says: "Hey give me my vase," in a monotone voice—an expressionless parody of her husband's ashes.

On the set she gorged on food in public all day long, completely unaware of what was going on around her. Alexis described her as having lived "in a blissful state of ignorance." She was constantly insulting everyone on the set, without realizing it. "It came naturally to her. She's not a bitch on purpose, she's just not happy." She compared her to Elvis because, like him, she didn't know when to stop.

The movie was a flop, receiving exceptionally low ratings. It was obviously made with no money and there was no plot other than to make fun of Anna. The audio is the best. The film was so low budget they couldn't even afford prop glasses. Anna gives someone a sip out of her martini glass and then chucks it on the pavement, as if it is a Greek celebration, but unfortunately the audio caught the sound of plastic bouncing off the concrete floor.

A review said that a "real Anna also makes a brief appearance, attempting to play herself and not totally succeeding." She was obviously at the height of her painkiller and eating addiction. On screen, and in the bonus-material interview afterwards, you can see she is uncomfortable in her own skin and can barely focus, never mind speak.

The comedy was described as "stupid" and a "waste of time" with Anna's weight-gain serving as the butt of all jokes. The teasing finally hit home and she decided to put an end to it. She said that radio jock Howard Stern was the final straw. He asked Anna to be on his show and then told her he didn't believe how much she said she weighed. He challenged that she was at least three hundred pounds and then pulled out a scale. He was like, ok, get on the scale and let's see how much you really weigh. Anna was so embarrassed and, to make matters worse, it was all caught on videotape for her reality show. They got listeners to call in and tell her they know she weighs three hundred pounds. They even bribed her with a bunch of jewelry to get her on the scale and she was really hurt. It was her humiliation that motivated her to lose all the weight: If she were thin, she could throw the jokes back in their faces.

After her second season finished, Anna kept a really low profile and then hit the media with her new thinner-than-ever figure. The story was huge; she managed to shock the world. No one believed her claims until they saw it for themselves. Even Larry King had her back on his show just to talk about her transformation, but she could not reveal how much she weighed because E! had an exclusive deal with her set for February 27.

Smug with her new body, Anna wanted to go back on the *Howard Stern Show* and get an apology for his previous remarks. He agreed to have her back on the condition she would leave her cameras behind. She took her crew anyway and but got only as far as the waiting room. The producers refused to allow her escorts through and she refused to go any further without them.

She screamed at Howard Stern telling him that he needed to apologize for calling her a porker and for making her weigh herself the last time she appeared. She attacked the producers, making an absolute scene because they would not let her on the show with her entourage. She insisted that her camera crew went everywhere with her at all times—they never left her side—but to no avail. Instead, Howard retaliated with, "Where were your camera crew when you lost all that weight?" and she stormed out fuming. As a result of this fiasco, Anna Nicole and her entire family were banned from ever coming back on the show.

So how did Anna manage to lose all that fat? If we believe everything she says then it would be entirely attributable to TrimSpa. What a joke! After a huge wave of public interest into her true methods of weight loss, Anna confessed that she simultaneously underwent a colon cleanse, during which she spent most of two weeks sitting on the toilet. This, she says, was in order to flush out all the especially stubborn areas of excess fat.

However, this still does not answer the question of where all the excess *skin* went. Anyone who has lost that much weight is guaranteed to have bulges, stretch marks, and flaps of unwanted skin hanging around, even if they *lived* in the gym. Despite being supplied with numerous fitness instructors by her producers, Anna certainly did not torture herself by doing any vigorous exercise, or in fact any exercise whatsoever—and she didn't need to.

The obvious answer to the great mystery is that she went for the most immediate solution that money can buy: surgery. She had to have had liposuction or a tummy tuck and then plastic surgery to cover up the scars. Britney Spears did it recently, so did Tara Reid, Star Jones and Al Roker from the *Today Show*. All the celebrities denied the real reason for their rapid weight loss at first, but the truth always comes out. Liposuction is the only way my sister could possibly have gone from the fat Anna Nicole to the flawless diet-pill model with a washboard stomach. Hello, she had no qualms putting silicone into her body countless times; there is no way she would have hesitated taking fat out of it.

Also this is not the first time that Anna would have had surgery. Aunt Elaine told me that she took Anna to have cosmetic dental surgery in the early 90's because she wanted a Hollywood smile. She also had extra thick veneers put on her teeth, which may account for the fact that the shape of her face changed. In later shots, when Anna smiled, she would flash a mouthful of glistening white teeth and her gum line was always visible.

Elaine was also with her when she had liposuction in 1993. Vickie wasn't even that big back then but she wanted to be thinner anyway. They were still not letting her work night shifts at the strip club and she put it down to her bulky figure. After the surgery, she couldn't leave the house for a while so her family all went to visit her lying in bed. There was no way I was going over there while she was in that state though. Everyone said that she was whining and miserable and that she would lash out at them at any given opportunity. Even though the pain was self-inflicted, she had to take it out on someone else.

Elaine went and visited her just after she came out of the hospital and brought back some photos for us to see: Anna was bed-bound and completely bandaged up. Then our dad came back with more photos once her skin had been uncovered and I was like, no wonder she's acting like that. It looked like she was in a lot of pain; her legs and thighs were all bruised and swollen where the surgery had been done. You have to remember that back then it was a lot more painful than it is these days.

If she had liposuction a decade ago, then why wouldn't she have it again a decade later, when she really needed to? If her weight loss was solely due to a strict fitness regime and by taking six TrimSpa pills a day then surely the process would have been featured on her show; she could even have sold a profitable weight-loss video.

The truth is that Anna has always taken the easy way out and surgery and drugs were handed to her on a plate. Ever since she left home, Anna has been on some form of drug and this time she replaced the kind that slow you down and make you slur your words for those that contain ephedrine or some other speed-based substance. She also dropped her incomprehensible Texas drawl and her speech became more pronounced because she wasn't doped up with opium-derived pills any more. She took elocution lessons and cleaned up her act for court; she even went to the extreme of putting on a suit and toning down her caked makeup. This façade didn't last long though and soon enough Anna went back to her old habits of debauchery and slurred words.

Anna's producers had been trying to get her to shed the pounds from the second the show started but, when she finally did, it was too late; she never got to show off her metamorphosed figure. With her perfect body, she started filming her show's third season but it got cut. Nevertheless E! could not bear to miss the opportunity to exploit her transformation. They made a deal with her to do a few extra episodes and aired them as specials.

However, Anna quickly found a new means to flaunt her new figure. In October 2003, she became a spokesperson for TrimSpa. Allegedly, she had already been taking the diet pills before they approached her. They had seen how much weight she had lost by taking their product and wanted her to represent their company. She claimed that, because of the diet pills, she had to force herself to eat and that, by taking six doses a day, she ended up losing more weight than she had intended. On *Larry King Live*, like a true spokeswoman, she repeated again and again that she no longer had an appetite and that people had to force her to eat something or she would just deteriorate. She insisted repeatedly that the pills had worked so well that she lost *too much* weight.

The pill's active ingredient is Hoodia gordonii, a natural appetite suppressant used by tribal hunters in South Africa. It also contains green tea extract, cocoa extract and circus niranganine. Anna claimed that the *only* side effect was having extra energy. She complained about this because it prevented her from lying in bed all day long. I think the real reason she had more energy than before was because, for a second, she had stopped taking Vicodin or Valium or whatever prescription drug she was on at that time. Perhaps she had no appetite because she had had gastric bypass surgery. The procedure is also called stomach stapling because it partially removes your stomach, making you less hungry. I guess we'll never learn the full truth, but everyone else was having it done at the time so why wouldn't she?

Anna remained the spokesperson for TrimSpa and stuck by her guns despite all the rumors and doubts that had been expressed about her honesty. TrimSpa said that they had had professionals check her body in order to prove that her body had never been touched. Considering the fact that there is evidence to prove that she had liposuction in 1993, I think the specialists need to rethink their jobs. In 2004, Anna even posed naked for a *Fashion Week* magazine to support her claim that her recent weight loss was the result of the diet product she was being paid to promote, and not the result of gastric bypass surgery or liposuction. The magazine's representative Roger Padilha was quoted as saying: "We asked her to recreate the famous Marilyn Monroe pose for the centerfold of our Icon issue. She thought it would be a good way to quash the rumors. I was there and can one hundred per cent vouch that she had no scars."

...At least none that couldn't be airbrushed. The thing is that, even if she was trying to prove she didn't have any incriminating scars, she had had plastic surgery to cover up them up anyway and, with today's technology, anything can be airbrushed. A lot of nude models have surgery, yet we don't see their scars in advertising campaigns.

TrimSpa would later be the cause of even more controversy when Joseph Farzam filed a lawsuit against Anna Nicole Smith and TrimSpa on behalf of three consumers. Janet Luna, Myra Luna and Yvonne Rodarte alleged the claims made by TrimSpa were false and misleading and could not be substantiated by any reliable medical evidence. They demanded that supporting documentation be provided. According to the plaintiffs, the magical rapid weight loss that TrimSpa X32 promised was a fabrication and the ingredients cannot cause the weight loss promised by TrimSpa's advertisements.

I spoke to Joseph Farzam and he informed me that since the case went public, many more angry customers came forward. He was contacted by dozens of people who claimed to have suffered side effects from taking the pill. One man said his wife had died, others had heart conditions, high blood pressure, hemorrhages, and one person asserted he had almost died. However, Farzam did not imply he had evidence that these symptoms were accurate. The issue in his case was about whether the pill worked or not and his clients were adamant that it did not. He also said that although he initially filed the case with three plaintiffs, he expected to be adding many more.

On January 4, 2007, the U.S. Federal Trade Commission fined TrimSpa's marketers Goen Technologies Corp., Nutramerica Corp., TrimSpa, Inc., and Alexander Szynalski—also known as Alexander Goen—$1.5 million. They were forced to pay the fine to settle FTC allegations that their weight-loss claims were unsubstantiated. The marketers had inadequate scientific evidence to support their advertising claims that TrimSpa caused rapid and substantial weight loss and that one of its ingredients, Hoodia gordonii, enables users to lose substantial weight by suppressing appetite.

According to an FTC statement, "The agreement also prohibits the marketers from making any claims about the health benefits, performance, efficacy, safety, or side effects of TrimSpa, Hoodia gordonii, or any dietary supplement, food, drug, or health-related service or program, unless the claims are true, not misleading, and substantiated by competent and reliable scientific evidence."

The FTC Chairman's public statement was plastered across all national media outlets: "You won't find weight loss in a bottle of pills that claims it has the latest scientific breakthrough or miracle ingredient. Paying for fad science is a good way to lose cash, not pounds."

Anna's death may well also be the end for TrimSpa. Photos of the contents of her fridge were leaked to the press showing cans of Slim Fast, TrimSpa's leading rival. Even though Anna had violated her contract, there was no longer anything they could do about it. Instead, TrimSpa announced it would be changing the direction of its advertising campaign, using the average person to promote the weight-loss pill rather than celebrity endorsement.

I knew the public would find out Anna's real involvement with TrimSpa sooner or later. I'm surprised it took this long for the truth to come out. I once showed a doctor the ingredients used in TrimSpa and he said there's no way it could help someone lose seventy pounds. He also said that, taken over a long period of time, the contents were more likely to do harm than good.

ANNA STOLE
MY BABIES!

The media had always expressed interest in my viewpoints on Vickie and the family and soon they began reaching out to me. I only did one magazine interview, which was unpaid, in March 2003. My sister, Amy, wanted to do some press on Anna because she was living in a homeless shelter and needed to make some money. At the time Virgie had a brain aneurysm and was in the hospital for three months. We were not sure that she was going to make it and Aunt Elaine was very concerned that the whole family should be told. No one could get hold of Anna as her whole entourage had been replaced since when Elaine worked for her. I contacted *Star* magazine so that they could publish the story about Virgie and Anna would hear about it from them. I gave them Elaine and Amy's contact details but, as I had been the one to initially contact them, they only wanted to deal with me. I agreed to talk to them on Amy's behalf as long as I remained anonymous.

They were so nice to me; they sucked me into telling them everything they wanted to know. They placated me by reassuring me that they would only use the information I wanted them to, my name wouldn't be mentioned, and that Virgie's illness would be their main story. So I, of course being the gullible person that I am, answered all their questions to their heart's content.

They wanted a photo and the only one we had where Amy didn't look too homely was of us with our cousin, Brandy, at a bar looking all dolled up. We sent the picture in to *Star* and they couldn't believe that Anna had relatives who were sober and had a full set of teeth. They thought that I looked more like Anna than the rest of her relatives and begged me to send in more photos so that they could use one for the front cover of the magazine. I really didn't want to be interviewed; I had only set it up for Amy and Elaine, so I stopped talking to them and refused to answer their calls. They wouldn't stop phoning me and even harassed my friends for more photos of me. I don't know how they got their numbers because I sure didn't give any more information out at that point. They even offered me a deal of up to $25,000, but I stood firmly by my answer.

"ANNA TRIED TO BUY MY BABIES!" These big letters jumped off the page at me, along with a huge photo of me right next to Anna's. Guess who is plastered across half of the magazine cover? Yours truly: Me. *Star* guaranteed that all of America now knew who I was and exactly what I looked like.

There are no big letters addressed to Anna telling her that her mother is dying in the hospital, nothing about Amy or Elaine, and no anonymity for me as they had promised. They screwed me over and blew up the wrong story. I told them I didn't want their money and I didn't want to be a part of the story, but they went ahead with it without a written agreement and without paying me. I was so furious about the front cover that I didn't even open the magazine at first. Then when I could finally bring myself to read the article, it quoted me as saying that I was devastated that Anna wanted to buy my daughters and take them away from me. It revealed my full name, Donna Faye Hogan, my children's names, and pretty much our exact address.

My children were distraught. Everyone in their school knew about the article. They were harassed by all their friends and schoolmates, as well as their teachers and the principal. They were already embarrassed by Anna's high-profile antics being exploited on every magazine cover and TV station. They did not want anyone to know that Anna was their aunt and yet here it was, plastered on the front cover of a magazine: Anna Nicole Smith was trying to take my children away from their mother. They came home crying, wanting to change schools because they were being teased.

I have three children, but the media mainly focused on my daughters as it was well known that Anna had always wanted girls. My youngest son, Brandon, was left out of the whole drama but my two daughters were deeply affected by it. Kayla was nine and Ashley was only eight when the story was published and the media especially had a field day with Kayla because of her name. I christened her Kayla Victoria because our other sister Amy's middle name is Kay, and I chose her second name after Vickie. Anna Nicole had always tried to get the family to name their children after her. There are three daughters in our family named Anna Nicole because she was so persuasive. She wanted me to do the same, but I drew the line and used Anna's real name, Victoria, as Kayla's middle name. Vickie insisted that it would sound better if her name came first, but ultimately I disagreed.

When the article came out, I immediately wanted to sue the magazine because my children were minors and so the press was not legally allowed to reveal information about them without my permission, especially not their names and where they lived. I started looking for someone to help me respond. I needed to be able to stop the press from ever manipulating me and releasing fake stories about me again, especially with the nerve to quote me as having told these lies. I knew I had to find someone to represent me and stand up to the press on my behalf; I had to learn how to play Anna's game.

I went to an attorney who offered to fight on my behalf but after a few months we dropped it as there was not enough evidence and it was too much of a hassle. Instead I found Karen Ammond to represent me. She is a nationally known New York-based publicist and she agreed to work with me immediately. Karen told me that we needed to get my side of the story out there—that this was the only way to protect my children and me from the lies being told about us. I knew that I had to start campaigning for the truth for the sake of my family. I mean, we're not all like Vickie or how Vickie portrays us.

From Karen I learned the media basically consists of exploited stories they think the public wants to hear. I was very upset that, no matter what you say, they can use the power of editing to convey what they want to get across. Most of the time, they will ask you a question and edit your answer so that it appears to be your response to something completely different. Not only do they edit your words on paper, they can even cut and add things on TV footage to make you tell whatever story they are pitching. By May, Karen helped me tell the story from my side.

I went on Fox News Channel, network television, CNN, *A Current Affair*, *Inside Edition*, *Entertainment Tonight* and started doing interviews with magazines in the USA and United Kingdom. With Karen's encouragement and support it was time I set the record straight. I was accomplishing exactly that! For the first time, I felt stronger and more optimistic and that perhaps there was hope for all of us to be viewed in the media not as "trailer trash" but a good, loving, hard-working family. I no longer felt depressed when a fabricated story appeared; I now knew how to counter that with the truth!

However, the battle was not yet over. We had heard that when I began to appear on television, Vickie's people called many shows and networks and threatened that if they interviewed me, Vickie would never appear on their show again. Even though Anna got attention and made money off anybody she could, she couldn't bear the thought of it happening to her.

Karen began to make calls to the show producers and, to my surprise and delight, many shows said they didn't care; they wanted me anyway! They trusted what I had to say and believed that I would only tell the truth. Anna was always known for "embellishing the truth" so it was not always in the interviewer's interest to question her. A few producers explained that they rarely did personal interviews with Anna, but simply ran footage of her latest red carpet disaster. So her threats meant nothing to them. The fact is, for Anna to make these threats was not a smart strategy on the part of her team. Any publicity is good publicity! She needed it, no matter how crazy she came off, the more press she got, the more money she could make from selling pictures and other outrageous things. By making these threats she could have damaged her relationship with the television shows.

Karen and I made sure that when I appeared on any media or in print I reported on the "facts" of the story, not hearsay. We researched as much as possible: what my sister had done and what harm her actions had caused this time! I wanted to be reliable. I didn't want to ever embarrass my children; I wanted them to be proud of me and our family and not allow any of this media with Anna to interfere with their life.

Not surprisingly, the media often told Karen and me that they never considered Vickie to be talented—simply an oddity that people were interested in. It was always, "What will she do next?" A producer from *A Current Affair* was not the only one to call Anna a "human train wreck." You can't help but stop and stare for a moment or two, but when you get close up there's no substance there. After witnessing a series of consecutive wrecks, you get bored. It's ironic that the most attention Anna ever got was when she died. It makes me so sad.

I can kind of understand why Anna got so fed up with the people around her. Everyone she met ended up selling their side of her story and it must be an awful life not being able to trust anyone around you. When my name started to appear nationally, I experienced what I imagine she must have gone through all the time. Everybody was jealous of me and treated me really badly, particularly our family.

Our sister Amy started writing blogs on any Internet message board she could find. In March 2006, she wrote on the VH-1 blog page:

> 2. my comment would be about my half sister anna nicole smith i have never spoken to anyone about my feelings toward anna but im sure you have heard about our other sister donna major head case its like she became obbsessed anyways i have some storys of my own would you like to hear them call or e-mail me 307-672-WXYZ [the original used Amy's real number]

> Posted at 3:09PM on Mar 1st 2006 by amy Hogan

She reposted this again at 3:25 and 3:26. Firstly, I think it's weird that she would write this on a public blog page for the whole world to see and secondly I cannot fathom why she would include her phone number for any freak out there to stalk her.

This is not the only time Amy has tried to badmouth me. Every time she found out that I was on television, she tried to sabotage me. She told the papers I was a druggie and a needle freak. Even my family came to check my body for track marks because of what she said.

After the American Music Awards (AMA) ceremony, the tabloids wanted to hear what I had to say about the way Anna had behaved. I really didn't want to do the interview but Amy was dying to be seen on TV and begged me to go on *Entertainment Tonight*. I agreed to do it and drove Amy and her husband to the show with me so that I could introduce her to the producers there.

When we got to the studio, I asked if Amy could sit down next to me and we could do the interview together, but the producers said that they only wanted me. During the entire interview, I could see Amy sitting off stage giving me go-to-hell looks. I told the interviewer I was exhausted and I wasn't sure I could go on and suggested that Amy take my place, but they refused. I told her I was trying but that wasn't good enough for my sister; she had a tantrum, swearing at me, and then stormed out.

The producers went outside to talk to Amy. They apologized for excluding her but said the show had already been preplanned. They needed some extra footage of me in action and offered to show a clip of Amy and me sitting at a table together. That way, other syndications would notice her and want her on the next time. Even Amy's husband encouraged her to do it, but Amy refused, shouting, "I don't fucking think so. It's all about you. You're just like Vickie."

I had to go and finish the interview. I apologized to the producers for Amy's behavior; I was so mortified that she was my sister. They reassured me that I was not responsible for her. At the end, Amy was waiting outside and again she started cursing at me: "First I have to put up with that nasty bitch Vickie and now I have to put up with you." She also attacked the producer I was talking to but it was too ridiculous for anyone to take seriously.

As Amy left, the producer said, "Bye Anna Junior." She told me Amy would never get anywhere because she had too much of an attitude. She was such a liability no one would want to risk having her on their show. I had to drive Amy and her husband back home and during the entire journey she told me how much she hated me and that I only wanted attention, like our sister.

On another occasion, a few months after ET, Amy called me up and apologized. I hadn't heard from her since the incident. Now, she told me she was really sorry. She said she had acted out because she was so desperate to be on the show herself. She asked me if I could get her an interview to talk about Anna so I called Karen and hooked her up with a small daytime show. Amy then somehow got hold of the producer's number and called him herself.

The producer called me right after and said, "You know what? She really hates you." At first she had told him I was like a parent to her and then she started spreading lies that I was a drug addict and other really awful things.

Another similar incident was when *Inside Edition* sent me a one-page document Amy had sent them, trying to destroy my reputation. It was obvious she was jealous because I had appeared on their show. She wanted to be a celebrity and was offended because I had landed myself a publicist when she couldn't.

Our father is even worse. I have heard people describe Donald as having a shit-eating grin on his face because everything he says is a lie. Donald is from Parkington, in north Texas. He grew up in the country, in the middle of miles of farmland and nothing else. His family was middle class. He was the only boy and was very spoiled. He was brought up thinking that he was the boss and better than everyone else.

My grandmother said that Donald's father was also abusive. He was an alcoholic, who beat the shit out of his son and sometimes even hit his wife. My father took after his father and probably a long line of abusive ancestors.

Just like his daughter, Donald has always needed to be the center of attention. He would try to be noticed by everyone, even strangers off the street. He would constantly mimic Clint Eastwood, with lines like, "Go ahead, make my day," and act out scenes from *Ernest Goes to Camp*, playing the goofy character down to a T. He always thought that he would make it as an actor one day; maybe that's where Anna got her ambition from.

When Anna became famous, Donald hated it. He came around my house one day, fuming. His home had been broken into and everything to do with Anna had been stolen: photos of her, home videos, magazines, her calendar, and small trinkets that had any value. That's not the only time his house was trashed. Almost every time Anna hit it big, his house would get ransacked. He hadn't been robbed for years, after there was nothing left to steal, but then in 2005 they broke into his shop instead.

When I was front-page news, Donald didn't like it either. During an interview with *Inside Edition*, I was sitting in the car with Kristen, the girl who was interviewing me. We were on our way to the country club to hear him sing. He is a really great country singer and I wanted to take Kristen to watch him perform. I called him to let him know that we were coming and he freaked out.

He thought we would bring cameras and so he blew up. He is such a con artist, he thought that somehow the government would find out what he was up to. He had been trying to file for disability for years, claiming that he couldn't work because his shoulder and back hurt. They eventually believed him and gave him the benefits.

Even though he has been employed for years and got a big check after my grandmother passed away, he continues to collect government money every month. He thought that if we brought cameras and filmed him working, the government would find out that he was able to work and would make him pay back all the disability money. He blew up. He refused to have us there even though I told him we didn't have a camera with us. He shouted, "Don't you fucking show up here," and threatened to cancel the whole gig.

CHAPTER 18

DONALD HOGAN

*O*ur father has been a scam artist his whole life. He has always had some kind of money-making scheme up his sleeve and it usually changes from month to month. One job that he has stuck to over the years, however, is as a weed dealer.

Donald owes child support for my sister Amy from years ago but he insists that he paid it all off. My mother is a drug addict and, instead of getting child support from Donald, she would collect bags of weed. He can't get his driver's license now because his record says that he still owes the money. What is he supposed to say in court? "Your Honor, I did pay the child support. I gave their mother weed."

My father had tons of other money-making schemes as well. He would drive his truck with his godfather and my Uncle Shelby directly to the local factories and steal gas. While I was living with him, I would see eighteen-wheelers pull up to the house and unload boxes of coke bottles. He filled the house with stolen goods to such an extent that there was no room for anything else.

While driving his eighteen-wheeler, Donald fell asleep at the wheel and rammed right into a truck. He didn't have a license and wasn't supposed to be driving, but somehow he and a friend invented a story and wrangled a $12,000 settlement out of it.

One of his other ventures was to go to downtown Houston and buy wholesale products such as knives and swords and sell them at marked-up prices. He also had a radiator shop and a rabbit, cockatoo and quail farm. He considered them investments and bought these animals as babies and bred them in his own yard. Once he decided that he had struck a goldmine by investing in a worm farm.

He got engaged to someone named Liz and opened a leather and bike shop, which he named after her. He called it "Liz's Leather Shop." Before Liz, he was seeing my Aunt Linda, Wanda's brother's ex-wife. Things in the South can get really incestuous sometimes. My father and Linda weren't blood-relations, but they were family. Linda had been married to my Uncle Shelby, for years. Once Linda divorced Shelby and my dad divorced his then-wife, Carole, the two of them shacked up. Donald is the epitome of *Hee Haw* country.

He was the most irresponsible father imaginable. Wanda could not fend for us and Donald would shamelessly watch his children starve. There were times our family was so poor, the children drank bean juice instead of milk.

My memories of my father have scarred me for life. I have tried to block out most of my childhood that involved him. My brother, Donnie, reminded me that Donald lived in the house with us until I was four and he was two. Up until he left, everybody would think I was mute because I refused to speak in front of my dad. The second I heard his car pull up outside the house I would be silent with fear.

He locked me in the freezing-cold garage every time I cried. He wouldn't let me out for hours and stopped my mother from trying to intervene. Usually my grandma would have to fight with him in order to get me out. If you ask Donald now, he denies it, saying, "Oh yeah, I put her out there once just to mess with her."

He has always picked on the weak ones. I never spoke, so I didn't pose a threat to him. He could do anything to me and I wouldn't have told anyone. After he moved out of our house, he lived in a motel for a while. Even after he got a house, every time I drove past the motel, I would be filled with hatred. I was relieved when it was demolished as I couldn't bear the memories it dredged up again and again.

Whenever we stayed with him, Donnie and Amy would sleep in one bed and I would have to share the other bed with my dad. Once, when Donnie asked if he could join us, my dad made some excuse why he couldn't.

I can still remember the times when my dad touched me inappropriately. Between the ages of five and nine he sexually abused me. He didn't do anything to my sister but I appeared weak to him and so he felt he could take advantage of me.

Everybody tried to warn my mother, Wanda, that she shouldn't leave her kids with Donald. Even her good friend, Abigail, told her he was up to no good, but Wanda saw him as a free baby-sitter. While we were with Donald, she could go out and have fun. When I was around nine, my dad got together with his underage girlfriend, Twila. She was always with him so he couldn't lay a finger on me during that period. I still felt uncomfortable around him though because he would undress me with his eyes and it creeped me out.

When I was sixteen, I finally confided in my mother. I couldn't stand being around Donald anymore. My mother just answered, "Everyone has to sacrifice something. This is your sacrifice. You need a place to live right? If you call the police, you'll all be separated." She knew that the one thing her children didn't want was to be split up and so that was her best threat.

On another occasion, when I told her what my father had done to me, all she could say was, "He really did that?" Through my sobs I confirmed that he had and she muttered, "Well, Abigail told me he did, I guess she was right." I said, "That's it?" And she got angry with me, "What else do you want me to say?"

My kids call her the psycho grandmother because she is so far gone. She took a lot of abuse from all the men she was with; for some reason she was only attracted to the violent type. One of her boyfriends sexually molested Amy and me when we were young girls, and the others treated our mother even worse. She took a lot of drugs when she was already emotionally unstable and now she will never be cured.

I get calls from the police from time to time asking me to take her in, but I never want to see her again. I have had her committed to mental asylums but they always release her eventually. She does not have medical insurance and there is only so long they can keep her for free. If I had any money I would put Wanda in an asylum permanently. I can't bear the thought of her roaming the streets. At one time she was living under a bridge. Then she went to Donnie, but refused to go into the house. She lived in her car outside his home for days on end without any food or exercise.

I don't understand why Donnie tries so hard to help Wanda after all she's done to him. She would stand back while our dad beat Donnie to a pulp. When Donnie was two months old, our father beat him up and, as a result, half his face was bruised black. He would beat all of us until we peed in our pants and Wanda did nothing to stop him.

Donald was good friends with Wanda's brother, Shelby. While our dad had his radiator shop, Shelby ran a paint and body shop and they shared the property. When Donnie was fourteen, he worked for Shelby for $10 per day. They would go off and have lunch, leaving Donnie at the shop with nothing to eat.

One time, Donald hid Shelby's handgun and accused Donnie of stealing it. As punishment, the two of them punched Donnie to the ground and then kept kicking his head. Donald got a wooden board, three feet long, two inches wide and one inch thick and beat Donnie with it until he couldn't stand up. This was not the only time Donald hid prized possessions of his for an excuse to beat Donnie up.

Donald got together with Twila when she was twelve. They were dating off and on, but then Twila married someone else. Her husband got her knocked up and then they split up. While she was pregnant with Chris, and at the height of her vulnerability, Donald took her back. He has always gone for the weak ones who have nowhere else to go. That's how he keeps them. They stayed together for over ten years because she was too scared to leave him. He said he would kill her if she did.

After our step-mom, Twila, left Donald, he lifted up the mattress and showed Donnie every single item he had accused my brother of stealing. He told Donnie that Twila had hidden it all to get him into trouble. Donnie didn't believe a word though, and his suspicions were later confirmed. He bumped into his step-mom in the grocery store and told her what his father had showed him. She sympathetically informed him, "It was all your daddy."

Donnie lived with our father off and on until he could afford to leave. He would run away when he couldn't take the abuse, but he always came back when he ran out of money. Donald only took him in because he was able to earn his keep. Donnie needed food and clothes for school and Donald said he would give his son the money if he worked all summer. He slaved away for his father and the week before school was about to start, Donnie asked for some money to buy school clothes. Donald refused, saying, "You have to get that stupid crap out of your head, you're not going to school." Donnie ran away again.

While Donnie was living with our dad, he would see him meditating. Donald would emerge in a trance with his eyes glazed over. Donnie asked him once what he was doing, and Donald told him, "I've got Satan on my side." Donnie believed he was the Devil incarnate.

They always had pets in the house. Once they had two puppies and Donald didn't want them around anymore. They were mutts and not worth anything. He told Donald they were going to stop them from breeding once and for all. Donald loaded the pups up in the truck, and drove Donnie two miles down the dirt road by their house. Donald stopped the car, got the puppies out and walked a few meters from the car. Then he handed Donnie a gun and commanded him to shoot his own puppies. Donnie refused and Donald shouted, "You coward! Show me you're a man." Donnie would never kill his own pets so Donald told him he could walk home, grabbed the gun back and shot the puppies himself.

On another occasion, Donnie witnessed our dad drowning his own cat as well as stray cats that got on his nerves. He also once hung his pet dog by the neck so that it could barely breathe and let it slowly choke to death.

Donald goes through women like paper. One of his wives was called Carole. She had a son, Clinton, who drowned in the river when he was twelve years old. Our father's reaction was inhuman. He said, "Guess what? Clinton drowned in the river. Ya know, I told that motherfucker he would be dead soon. I thought it would be a needle hanging out of his arm but drowning is just as good." Donnie was so upset by what had happened he couldn't even utter a response.

Donald has no scruples. Even though Donnie had done everything to stay out of his way, Donald continued to mess with his livelihood. Donnie was hired for a construction job and when he got there his father had beaten him to it with his crew. He stole his son's job right from under his nose and it was Donnie's kids who were made to suffer.

Donnie is now a mixed martial arts fighter. After being beaten up every time his father had a bad day, he decided to learn to defend himself once and for all. Let Donald try to beat him up now! Donnie doesn't drink a drop of alcohol and he's a good father to his twin boys and wife, Micki.

Donnie has made sure that both of his eleven-year-old boys, Donnie and Danny Ray Hogan, have never met their grandfather.

They know that he is an evil person but Donnie has protected them from any of the lurid details. In 2000, Donnie and his family moved to another state and he hasn't spoken to his father since.

When my kids were little, I tried to give my father a second chance. Up until 2004, I attempted to talk to him and overlook the past. He had stopped drinking and I thought he had changed. With my parents' history and the rest of my dysfunctional family, I wanted some stability in my life and I thought he might be able to provide that. I now know that he will never change.

THE GREEK TYCOON

*I*n 2004, I was asked to be on *A Current Affair*. They filmed me being interviewed for TV and they did a publicity photo shoot near where I live. I hated it and began to understand what it was like for a model to be stared and snickered at. I took off my shoes for the shoot and somebody actually stole them. I couldn't believe it; why would anyone want my used high heels?

My interview was syndicated in England and was seen by Maurizio, a Greek tycoon living there at the time. That very day he had his secretary call the producer of the show and get my e-mail address. She e-mailed me with his number and asked me to call him. She sent his profile, with all the details about his background and wealth so that I would believe he wasn't just a psycho off the street. It showed that he has more money than you could imagine and that he owns hotels all over Europe. I was hesitant at first but I was having problems at home with my ex and the media stalking me so I thought there couldn't be any harm in just a phone call. I spoke to him and his first words were, "It's about time." He had never had to wait two weeks for a woman to call him. He had so much money he thought he could buy everything he wanted, including me.

Two days later I had one hundred long stem pink roses delivered to my door. It was the biggest bouquet I had ever seen. I told him that I had to get away from my house because at the time I was constantly being harassed by the tabloids. There were people with cameras everywhere and they had no limits as to what they would do. I had to call the police constantly and was often scared in my own home with my kids. When I told him this he told me to pick any place I wanted to go on vacation. My best friend and neighbor April and I chose Miami. I knew that the *Splash* journalist lived there, but I love it there anyway. I told him the kids had not been before and so he paid for all of us to go; he even paid for April and her children. He sent me thousands of dollars all the time. Before I left he sent me large sums of money and when I was there he booked us a two-bedroom suite for a month and sent us spending money once we got there.

He made me promises of gifts and he wanted to get me a passport so that I could move to Greece. For a while I toyed with the idea of moving to Athens to live with him. I know that it's ridiculous but it was so tempting to just move away from all the craziness and live in Greece with a millionaire. He promised me more than Anna would ever have and it was very enticing.

Then I got to know him better and I realized that Greek men are scary, at least this one was. I agreed to meet him at the Houston International Airport for a drink. We spoke for a while, but that was the last time I saw him. He told me that Greek men are very possessive, as if it was complimentary, but it made me feel entrapped before I had even committed to anything.

He bought me a car and had the Mercedes dealership call me, but I never went to pick it up. He tried to ply me with gifts, but I didn't want to be bought. He said a gift is a gift, a promise is a promise, but I didn't want anything more from him. He was really threatening to me. He told me that Greek men get what they want and I did not want to live my life in fear and under his control.

I was having problems with my ex, Robert, and Maurizio wanted to punish him. It was a time when the media were everywhere. I had just done the *Current Affair* interview and a high-profile photo shoot at the Memorial City Mall for them as publicity. In a small town that sort of attention is always blown out of proportion and everyone wanted my autograph. My house was always surrounded with fans and I even had the police and FBI wanting to meet me because of the televised show.

Even though we were already splitting up, Robert was jealous because I was receiving all this attention. He didn't want me talking to any other men and, when we watched the interview on TV, he got the glass coffee table in front of the couch and threw it on the floor so that it smashed into thousands of pieces. He yanked the phone cord out so that no one could call me and he was really aggressive towards me. Even when he was no longer living in my house he would break in so that I had to call the police. He worked out of state, but he would come over with the excuse that he was there to see his kids and that I couldn't stop him. Even my friends stopped coming around for a while because they were scared that he would turn up.

I told Maurizio what Robert was like because I wanted to get away from it all. I didn't want anything bad to happen to Robert but the Greek would not listen. He hired two big guys in a white SUV go to Robert's house in front of all the neighbors. While everyone was watching, they threatened Robert, warning him not to have any contact with me again. I was angry he had done that because I definitely hadn't asked him to and my problems with my ex were none of his business. Instead he got mad at *me*, telling me that when he decides to do something I should stay out of his business. He said everybody knew not to cross him.

Maurizio was very powerful and possessive and, even though during the whole time we were talking I had only met him once, he knew everything about me. He kept a track of me all day long. I had no idea at the time but he was having me followed and knew exactly what I had been doing. When I went to Miami, he knew I had chosen that destination because I wanted to see another man. He knew what my plans were even before I made them and it really unnerved me. Maurizio phoned me up and accused me of cheating on him even before I had. I had no idea how he found out, but there was only one explanation—he had a private investigator tailing me the entire time. I felt trapped and knew that I had to get away from him so I stopped answering his calls and rejected any of his gifts from then on.

My sister Amy and I have always had gifts bought for us by men. I have had two cars given to me, as has my sister. We have both received uncountable expensive gifts and marriage proposals, but I have never been able to fall for the rich guy. I could never marry for money and sometimes I wonder why this is. If Anna could marry a man she had never lived with then why can't I? It's not like I fall for the humble saint. I still end up with the wrong type of men, who control and abuse me, but, instead of being a rich abuser, he's a poor one. If I went for a billionaire and was treated badly at least I'd end up with a nice house. I'm not that type of person though; unfortunately, I could never marry for money.

CHAPTER 20

TRAIN WRECK

*"Anna continues to garner ratings.
Like a train wreck, people want to stop and stare;
they are curious yet appalled at what they see."*
—CURRENT AFFAIR TV PRODUCER

*I*n November 2004, Anna was the target of virulent media attacks, accusing her of getting on stage at the American Music Awards so drunk she couldn't speak. As she walked into sight, Anna waved her hands in the air and, once she arrived at the microphone, she caressed her body from bottom to top. The first line she delivered was, "DO YOU LIKE MY BODY?" as she winked at the audience and stroked her breasts. This was followed by some incoherent words intended to flatter Kanye West, whom she was introducing. An uncomfortable silence ensued while Anna stood there with her hands up in the air again, flaunting her new figure. Eventually the music came on and Kanye was able to deliver his performance.

She was so incomprehensible that the next day, satirical website *BrokenNewz* reported: "The CIA 'gave up' yesterday trying to interpret a speech given by Anna Nicole."

"'We're baffled,' said an (of course) anonymous CIA analyst. 'This is more mysterious, more puzzling than anything from bin Laden or al-Zarqawi. The only thing we can say is that she wasn't speaking in Arabic.'

"An AWA poll taken immediately after the show reflected Smith's confusing speech. 79% of viewers said they 'more clearly comprehended' West's ensuing performance than Anna's bizarre podium antics.

"'We picked up a couple *bitches* and *mutha$#@&ers* from Mr. West,' said another CIA analyst. 'But Ms. Smith gave us nothing to work with.'

"'The only information the CIA did learn was that Smith 'set back the cause of blondes another decade or so.'"

The producers of the show wanted Anna, and they got her as she really is. The funny thing about it all is that Howard K. Stern publicly denied that she was drunk or under the influence of drugs.

It took Anna five days to respond to any accusations: "We thought everything was fine. I went offstage. I said, 'Oh my gosh, I missed the line.' The guy said, 'Don't worry about it, it's fine. The crowd went crazy.' I did interviews before and after. I took pictures with everybody. I just had a wonderful time. Then we left. It wasn't until the next morning when we woke up. Then we got all these crazy phone calls. Howard's phone was, like, booked solid. It was, like, crazy. Everyone out of the blue is calling, calling, calling."

Howard blamed her slurring on her eyesight: according to him she couldn't read as far as the teleprompter. Anna used the excuse that she was nervous. She needed the two bodyguards to hold her up so that she would not trip over a cable—it was dark.

The same day, Anna did an interview with Kevin Frazier for *Entertainment Tonight*. She gave an honest account of her difficulties coping with her late husband's death and the legal war that ensued. She finally admitted to her life-and-death battle with prescription drugs. Although she had always publicly denied having an overdose, she confided in Frazier: "I actually went into a coma, you know. I almost died. And I had to learn how to walk again and all this and that." She said it was, "Horrible, horrible, horrible because I couldn't walk. I had to rehabilitate myself. And then they took the nurse away, so there I was crawling—crawling to the bathroom and stuff."

She described her experiences on drugs: "You just, like, leave your body. It's, like, unexplainable. It's like—like one time I went to the park, my friend took me to the park, and I thought I was walking on stilts." However, she told Frazier her addiction was a habit of the past. She no longer took drugs and barely drank.

After the AMA award ceremony, Anna shrugged it off. "People thought I was drunk and on drugs. I'm not having a melt-down. I'm not losing it, America! I'm fine. I'm okay."

Frazier was asked to respond to her behavior and, like the rest of the world, he questioned her sobriety. Even during their exclusive interview, she made him feel uncomfortable. He said, "there was definitely something wrong with Anna.... I'll be honest with you. Something is going on. But, at the same time, I wonder...is she crazy like a fox? Because is there any better self-promotion?"

He's right. There's no doubt that Anna's bizarre behavior attracted her more attention than if she had walked on stage in a straight line and coherently delivered her lines. But, there is no way that her drug addiction was behind her, no matter what statements she made to the public.

In December 2004, Anna was invited to the VH1 *Big in '04* awards. She won the Big Makeover award for her slimmed-down body. On stage she jokingly held up a red giant bra that she "used to" wear when she was heavier. Again she wanted to show off her figure by taking off her top in front of the cameras but a security guard caught her just in time and she was escorted off the stage. Backstage, she continued where she left off, posing for the cameras with actress, Brigitte Nielsen, fondling her own breasts.

In March 2005, the MTV Video Music Awards decided that Anna's notorious performance was exactly what they wanted at their event. They flew her in, along with Striptease Aerobics queen, Carmen Electra, to help host the event at Sydney's Luna Park. Along with the legendary surfer, Kelly Slater, Anna presented the Video of the Year award to the band, The Dissociavites.

While the lead singer, Daniel Johns, made his way to the stage, Anna spoofed Janet Jackson's wardrobe malfunction by pulling down her dress to reveal both breasts, each covered with the MTV logo. While topless, she jumped on Daniel Johns and wrapped both her legs around his waist.

As if that hadn't attracted enough attention, Anna volunteered to follow Carmen Electra's lead and strip for her audience. "If y'all want me to strip, let me know." When no one responded, she pulled down her dress and exposed one of her breasts again at the press conference later that night. This time round there was no MTV sticker covering it.

The following month, Anna was invited to Tennessee's Grand Ole Opry, Nashville's prestigious country-music event. In the middle of a dance, Anna abandoned her partner and did her own routine; she parted the slit in her dress to reveal her panties and, at one point, her boob fell out. The crowds looked on in horror as she shimmied around shaking her breasts.

On July 2, 2005, Anna was asked to present at Live 8 in Philadelphia but, following her appearance on stage, the charity event sued TrimSpa for her behavior. On December 1, 2005, Live 8 filed legal documents claiming that the diet pill's spokeswoman, Anna Nicole Smith, had besmirched their reputation. She had attended the music benefit dressed in a shiny pink vest held together by a string across her cleavage.

According to the U.S. District Court in California, the charity organization, Live 8, accused Anna of being "scantily clad" and "intoxicated" and said that she displayed "unbecoming and erratic behavior."

In the lawsuit, the organizers of Live 8 stated that Anna was dressed in an outfit: "totally inappropriate for a broadcast that would be seen by millions of people in the United States and then rebroadcast throughout the world." They also alleged that she was intoxicated at the time of her appearance and that she "damaged Live 8's reputation and goodwill in the entertainment industry by her unbecoming and erratic behavior."

Had they never heard of Anna Nicole Smith before? It's not like she had the reputation of a saint and, with one news-breaking story after the next of Anna flashing her breasts, her behavior was hardly unpredictable. In my opinion, compared to her prior appearances, she was well-behaved at Live 8. She didn't try to strip and considering it was over a hundred degrees on the day of the event, she wasn't even that skimpily dressed. What did they expect her to wear—a turtleneck?

Then there are accusations that she ruined Live 8's repu-tation. Live 8 is a charity organization that supports the starving and impoverished. What on earth were they doing adver-tising a diet pill? It seems slightly ironic to me that they let TrimSpa sponsor the charity event in the first place.

Again, Howard K. Stern was there to defend his client. He publicly responded to the accusations, saying Anna was neither drunk nor inappropriately dressed. He told the press that the concert organizers pre-approved Anna's attire: "We were aware that it might be perceived as revealing. I was told that she looked beautiful and not to change a thing."

The real reason that TrimSpa was being sued was because they had failed to pay the $320,000 fee for four 30-second advertising spots. Live 8 filed a claim seeking in excess of $500,000 in damages from TrimSpa to cover both the cost of the unpaid advertising spots and to compensate for Vickie's conduct. Although I think they added Vickie to the claim gratuitously so that they could sue for more money.

All in all, Anna's guest appearances since her weight loss caused quite a stir. At least Puff Daddy saw the humor in it, stating: "The world would be a boring place without Anna Nicole Smith."

In her defense, not all of Anna's escapades were profane. She used her fame to do good, too: campaigning against fur and modeling for plus-sized clothing. Even during the times Anna was heavily overweight, she always had a lot of character and has inspired a lot of people to pursue their ambitions. As I've mentioned, it's easy to ridicule her. But, you have to look at her positive qualities, too, like what she has achieved for herself and why people are so obsessed with her.

From as early as 1995, the plus-sized clothing company, Lane Bryant, used Anna Nicole as their spokeswoman. The label had been heavily criticized for using thin models to advertise its clothing for larger women and, in order to save their image, they knew they had to take steps to rectify this. Anna Nicole was the perfect candidate to pave the way for other larger models. She was one of the highest-weighing *Playboy* models and yet had been awarded Playmate of the Year, proving that she could pull off being larger than the average-sized model. She looked beautiful in their advertising campaign and walking down the runway for three years running. Lane Bryant subsequently hired other plus-sized personalities such as Kathy Najimy, Queen Latifah and Carré Otis, showing their market that you do not have to be thin to look good.

After successfully modeling for other labels, Anna decided to create her own. In 2004, she joined forces with the international designer, Von Dutch, creating a clothing line with their label called "Tex-Sex." The title combined both her Texas roots and sex-symbol status and, on August 30, she unveiled a fashion showcase at Magic Marketplace in Vegas, with T-shirts saying "Skinny Bitch" and "Guess who's Back?" This collaboration with a southern California-based label was obviously another of Anna's attempts to get her face back into the Hollywood spotlight.

In the same year, she modeled in advertisements for the animal rights group PETA. She spoofed Marilyn Monroe singing, "Diamonds Are a Girl's Best Friend," dressed in a pink satin dress surrounded by a group of tuxedoed suitors. The campaign was retitled: "Gentlemen Prefer Fur-free Blondes."

They quote Anna: "To kill an animal for a coat is crazy. My late husband gave me two fur coats years ago, but I've never worn them, and I never will. I'm a HUGE animal lover and have three dogs, Sugar Pie, Marilyn, and Puppy. How can anybody who calls themselves an animal lover wear fur? What they do to these animals to make fur coats should be illegal." Other celebrities such as supermodel Giselle Bündchen, Sarah Jessica Parker and Charlize Theron followed suit, campaigning for the cause.

If you saw what they do to the poor animals for their fur, you would have to look away. They are trapped, drowned, and beaten to death in the wild; and gassed, strangled, and electrocuted on fur farms. An anonymous man on the PETA website demonstrates how an animal's neck is broken and it is then left twitching on the floor. They also show a seal being beaten and left to suffocate in its own blood.

That business is cruel beyond imagination and Anna succeeded in making a lot more people aware of what is going on. Anna has a following that reaches the most destitute parts of America because that is where she came from. She was a white-trash Texan that people could relate to. She was beautiful but not intimidating, like most other celebrities, and when she stood for something a lot of people followed her lead.

In another ad the following year, Anna posed with her dogs in a campaign against Iams dog food for their cruelty to animals. She posed in a photo, declaring: "For the love of dogs, boycott Iams! These tests are not required by law, and animals shouldn't live in squalor and misery for the sake of Iams' profits." According to PETA, Iams conducts lab experiments on animals. The dogs and cats are confined to small, barren cages for up to six years; the dogs' vocal cords have been surgically cut out so that they can't bark; and dogs have been force-fed vegetable oil through tubes inserted down their throats. It is shocking that these kinds of conditions still exist, and without celebrity endorsement most people would not pay any attention to what is going on. Anna was an animal lover, she always surrounded herself with animals and I think her support for them was truly admirable.

Anna's love of animals was so great, that PETA, the leading organization for protecting animals, issued the following statement after Anna's death and asked me to use it in my book:

> *PETA is extremely upset by the news of Anna Nicole Smith's untimely death. She was a great friend to animals and used every opportunity to speak out against senseless cruelty. We always thought Anna Nicole was a perfect fit for PETA because, just like us, she not only hated cruelty to animals and loved her dogs but also couldn't be ignored, and no matter what people thought of her, they always had an opinion, one way or another. A long-time vegetarian who had slimmed down into a stunning beauty when she stopped eating meat, Anna Nicole spoke out against Iams because of its cruel animal tests, spoke up for baby seals bludgeoned to death for their fur in Canada, and posed as Marilyn Monroe in one of PETA's most striking ad campaigns, "Gentlemen Prefer Fur-Free Blondes." It is a tragedy when anyone passes away before their time, but with Anna Nicole, animals have lost a true hero and PETA has lost a good friend. We will miss her.*

CHAPTER 21

NATIONAL ENQUIRER
COLUMNIST

*"You know, what better way to
get my words out there. And you know,
another way to look at it is what better
way to get an education, right?"*
—ANNA NICOLE SMITH

In 2005, *National Enquirer* decided to revamp their gossip magazine and they found just the person to do it. On April 7, Anna Nicole Smith was announced as their new columnist. They probably saved a lot of money by hiring Anna to write about herself instead of paying her ex-lovers and family a fortune for exclusives. She was allowed to write anything she wanted. We all know that the *National Enquirer* has a reputation for inventing stories and exaggerating its headlines and so Anna had a lot of leeway to trash anyone she pleased.

When questioned about this career move in an interview, she answered, "I know I'm not a writer. I don't even know how to spell. You know, what better way to get my words out there. And you know, another way to look at it is what better way to get an education, right?" Anna once saw a poll showing that there were a lot of people who didn't like her and she thought that by writing a column she could change their minds.

Anna had no idea how to write, but she could get anybody to do that for her. All she had to do was tell them who to write about and, most of the time, they probably made it up on her behalf.

She did well to land herself a job getting paid to trash other people. Who better to dish celebrity trivia than a woman who had been made a celebrity by trivial gossip? She did a great job of mocking Kirstie Alley for trying to steal her job as a weight-loss representative; Michael Jackson for wearing pajamas to court; and, all the while, she was able to mock herself.

She praised Demi Moore and Ashton Kutcher's relationship, writing, "Go, Demi! Go, Ashton! Go, age difference!" She also offered up some sympathy for celebrity journalist, Pat O'Brien, who had recently checked himself into rehab for an alcohol problem. "Rehab sucks," she wrote. "There's no special treatment." She'd know.

Then Anna used her column to attack me, claiming that as far as she was concerned we are not related. Anna thought I had made up the fact she treated her family badly in recent years but the truth is it doesn't take a genius to point that out. How could anybody possibly think she was friendly to a family she no longer spoke to?

A journalist approached Anna at Grand Central Station in New York, while she was launching her new column. He asked her what she thought of me saying that she had abandoned her family. To begin with, she can't have liked being interrupted from receiving the adoration of autograph-hunting fans and, secondly, the question he asked must have hit a nerve: By removing any association with her family, she was trying to be someone she was not.

Instead of acknowledging her family, she used her column to publicly denounce me as her sister. In the middle of the page she titled her red heart-shaped piece, "My so-called 'sister' is a user-loser". She wrote, "This lady may be my biological dad's daughter, but she's not my sister. My biological dad left me when I was a kid. I didn't even know he had another daughter until I was an adult. Until after I became a celebrity. To this day, I've never seen her. I don't know her. But, somehow, this lady has the nerve to do interviews about me...."

She didn't take this opportunity to write that while she was desperately looking for the father who left her as a child, I was living in his house. Nor does she tell her readers that when she found her father and spent a lot of time with him, I was there too. She says she had never met me but I have photos of us together and, unlike most of our family's relationships, there were times when we got along.

In the column, Anna wrote directly to me, "Donna, stop saying you're my sister. Stop doing interviews about me. Why don't you try to make it on your own and stop using my name?" If I could choose to live my own life, independently from her, I would. She didn't realize that her outlandish antics meant that every time she was plastered on a newspaper cover, journalists came to me for answers and that, if I didn't tell them what they wanted to know, they were going to make it up anyway.

Anna called me a "user-loser," but she was actually the one who would use anyone she could to get either fame or money. In some ways we were very similar but with Anna there were no limits to what she would do. She questioned my motives and wrote that I must be in it for the money when I had never been paid for one magazine story that I was quoted in. I may have found other ways to make a bit of cash out of being Anna's sister but, for over ten years, Anna fought to make millions for being married to a wheelchair-bound billionaire, sixty-three years older than her. Anna turned the term "using" into a full-time profession.

She wrote, "Who do you think she talked about on those shows? You guessed it—me." Who else would I talk about? She was one of the most famous women in the world; surely she expected to be talked about. Anna thrived on being in the limelight and, if no one was talking about her, she would have complained a hell of a lot more.

The thing about Anna was she could work any situation to her advantage. No matter what story came out about Anna Nicole Smith, her publicity team could turn it into a news headline that she would ultimately cash in on. Whether she chose to trash me or Elaine or her mother or even Bobby Trendy, believe me, Anna was always making the most money.

CHAPTER 22

THE LAST WILL

> *"Everything else that I have ever*
> *given her to be hers now and forever.*
> *I love you."*
> —J. HOWARD MARSHALL II

The world had never seen what J. Howard Marshall looked like until Anna's Aunt Elaine went public with a shocking home video that had been recorded on the morning of December 25, 1992, eighteen months before they got married. Anna is in a gorgeous bathrobe with her hair up—guess what was holding it there? Elaine told me that at times she would use a thong instead of a hair tie.

It is Christmas time and so Anna is exceptionally excited. The tape is crazy. With the camera rolling, she stands alongside J. Howard in his wheelchair as he opens a series of unusual, carefully selected presents from her. And then she gives him a figurine of some sort. I was like, what is she doing? What is her point with the gifts? Does he collect them? But then I knew: it was a ploy. Anna shows him a huge ceramic display on the floor. It is the Last Supper. She asks him, "What do you think?" He said it's nice. She says, "And…." He says, "And I like it." She says, "And…." He replies, "I don't know what else to say."

She is staring him down and he says, "What do you want me to say?" Then, like a scene from a different movie, Anna says, "Go ahead, Howard, start talking—what you told me last night." She blatantly tries to get him to deliver a verbal will, stating, "I, Howard Marshall, being of sound mind, express this, my last will and testament. I give you everything I have." But the ruse backfires. Whatever he may have said the night before, off camera, he now promises her nothing beyond "everything else that I have ever given her."

He says, "Oh, yes." Then he proceeds to state that she should get what he has already given her but he mentions nothing about anything else. He says slowly, "I, Howard Marshall, being of disposing mind, express this my last will and testament to Vickie Nicole, shall receive the house—which she calls the ranch—and the townhouse and her Mercedes automobile and everything else that I have ever given her to be hers now and forever. I love you."

Even though he has not said anything to acknowledge he will give her any additional money, half of his estate or even anything more than he has already given her at this point, Vickie is contented by this statement.

She may have persuaded him to hand over his estate the night before, when she was preparing him for the recording, but while the camera was rolling, nothing of the sort was mentioned. Maybe she wasn't thinking clearly that day or maybe she didn't realize what was necessary for her to have the claim to J. Howard's fortune. Either way, all her manipulative tactics were in vain. In fact this ploy did her more harm than good, when the tape was found a decade later.

The tape continues with Anna rewarding J. Howard for reciting his will. She makes the Old Man close his eyes while she carries a huge framed picture of herself into the room. The poster is so big, it out-sizes the real Anna. She holds it in front of her and shows it to the camera. The photo shows Anna posing provocatively in sexy Santa underwear. When J. Howard opens his eyes, he smirks and says, "That's a little sexy, dear." The Christmas scenario seems highly inappropriate, considering Daniel is an eight-year-old child, watching his mother give her geriatric boyfriend a semi-nude photo of herself.

Then she takes J. Howard outside and they ride four-wheelers for a while. She even rides around with him attached to the back while she is driving. It looks like he is hanging on for dear life. It is so funny and cute, in a weird way. But obviously another one of her manipulative tactics: She was either trying to show him the time of his life, so that he would be sure to hand over all of his money, or she wanted him to have a heart attack!

Despite all these attempts to appease him, he says nothing about leaving her half of his estate and never mentions any money. If she was going to con him into leaving his estate to her, shouldn't she have had cue cards or something for him to read? She didn't have him say what she needed him to say, and that was half of his estate.

Despite this, Vickie lied. In court she swore that J. Howard had left her half of everything he had. She promised that his verbal agreement had been filmed and that she would be able to prove it if the tape could be found. However, when the tape was eventually discovered, there was no mention of J. Howard's money and he certainly did not say anything about Anna receiving half of everything he owns.

Vickie's greatest fear was always the possibility of the videotapes from that Christmas and their pre-honeymoon trip to Bali resurfacing. What is a very weird coincidence is that in 2005, at about the same time the tapes were released to the public, the story broke that J. Howard had secretly gone to a sperm bank back in 1995 to get his fertility tested. Anna had always wanted a daughter and so J. Howard got tested to see if he could provide her with children. Melvin had taken him as they did not want E. Pierce to find out what they were up to.

Two months after it became publicly known that J. Howard was still fertile in 1995, just before he died, and that he had *possibly* had his sperm frozen, Anna became pregnant with a girl.

THE SUPREME COURT STEPS IN

"One of the most mysterious and esoteric branches of the law of federal jurisdiction."
—JUDGE RICHARD POSNER

Even though Anna had won her bankruptcy case in California, the outcome of her federal trial had still not been decided. Anna may have been awarded $474,754,134, but that did not mean that she would see one cent of it. Anna did not care. She was so excited that she had beaten E. Pierce, she dropped all her charges against him in the Texas probate court.

E. Pierce, on the other hand, had no intention of letting Anna off and instead pursued his counterclaims against her with even more vigor. The Texas probate court conducted a jury trial that lasted more than five months with forty-four witnesses including everybody involved from J. Howard's staff to family friends, E. Pierce and Anna.

Unlike the California court findings, the Texas jury did not buy into Anna's accusations against Pierce. For them the issues were relatively simple. Did the late J. Howard Marshal II intend to give Anna Nicole any gifts in addition to the more than $6.7

million he gave her? And did his son E. Pierce Marshall interfere with the giving of such gifts?

Anna had no witnesses to support her claims; instead, her legal team tried to spin a conspiracy theory that focused more attention on J. Howard's estate planning than on Anna's vague and unsubstantiated claims. After the trial, the jurors in Houston said they had seen through this strategy during the case.

Almost everyone involved in J. Howard's estate plan had been accused of conspiring against him but there was also a lot of evidence to confirm that J. Howard controlled his estate plan until the end. Almost all of the forty-four witnesses testified that J. Howard's wishes were fulfilled. Although he had asked for hypothetical prenuptial agreements and trusts to be drafted, he ultimately blew most of them off for tax reasons.

J. Howard examined a number of strategies for funneling money to Anna Nicole Smith and, ultimately, decided that forming a company to promote Anna Nicole Smith's career was the most practical approach. The company was formed, although Anna Nicole Smith refused to go along with the plan. Ironically, Anna married one of the country's most successful business executives and then didn't listen to his advice concerning her business.

To Anna's horror, in December 2001, the court announced that she had no right to J. Howard's estate and that she had to reimburse E. Pierce's legal fees totaling $541,000. In addition, E. Pierce could collect an additional $100,000 in legal fees from Anna each time she filed an unsuccessful appeal. The Texas Probate Court also declared that they had jurisdiction over this case and it could not be heard anywhere else.

The media ate up her loss: "Anna Nicole Smith has something new to cry about. Jurors didn't buy her story that she was promised half of her late husband's wealth and didn't buy her courtroom act, which frequently included crocodile tears."

"Today a Houston judge gave Smith something to really cry about. In addition to losing her case the judge today signed a Final Judgment ordering that Smith pay the legal fees of her late husband's rightful heir, E. Pierce Marshall."

This was around the same time the bankruptcy case was transferred to the U.S. District Court to be reassessed. Anna won her case there and was awarded $88 million. However, the Ninth Circuit Court of Appeals reversed this decision and ruled that the Texas Probate Court had exclusive jurisdiction over any of her claims and J. Howard's will. That was it. Vickie's big win had been reversed.

The Ninth Circuit said that the federal judge in California who ruled in Anna's favor in 2002 should not have heard the case. E. Pierce was overjoyed: "After nine years of litigation, I'm very pleased by the judgment issued by the Ninth Circuit upholding my father's wishes regarding disposition of his assets."

Despite losing her court case, Anna was not going to give up without a fight. She had already been in court for ten years of her life, how much of a difference would a few more years make? Anna appealed their decision, but it was to no avail; the Ninth Circuit would not budge.

Anna needed backup quickly. She had one last attempt at getting her hands on millions of dollars, and she knew exactly who to turn to for help: the President.

On February 28, 2006, the Supreme Court of the United States was the site of a spectacle unlike anything that had ever been seen before on those hallowed grounds. Against all expectation, the highest and most powerful court in America had agreed to hear Anna Nicole Smith's case. They reasoned that their support was due to an interest in protecting the federal court jurisdiction in state probate disputes.

A crowd of cameramen, reporters, and spectators were on hand to watch her arrival. And they got an eyeful. Anna had been undergoing another round of remodeling. She looked breathtakingly gorgeous, concealing most of her face with black Onassis sunglasses and long platinum hair extensions.

The Bush administration sent the Solicitor General, the second-highest legal officer in the nation, to support her lawyers' arguments—an almost unheard-of action. Usually his job would be to argue on the side of the Government of the United States. However, in this case the Solicitor General's assistant, Deanne Maynard, fought on behalf of Anna Nicole Smith, as if he were defending his country.

Her plan triumphed and on May 1, 2006, The Supreme Court ruled unanimously: 9-0, in Anna's favor. They overturned the Ninth Circuit's verdict on jurisdictional grounds. Because Anna's claim was not about J. Howard's will, his estate or any other probate matter, they decided that her case could not be tried in the Texas probate Court.

Anna had smartly changed her tactics long ago and by now the issue was no longer about annulling or changing J. Howard's will but about E. Pierce's fraudulent actions. The case Anna was filing was a personal attack on E. Pierce for making decisions behind his father's back, of conspiring to keep her from seeing her husband, and for interfering with her inheritance and the gifts that were given to her.

After months of hearings and waiting around, Anna won the Supreme Court trial but it still didn't put any money into her pocket; it only sent the case back to the lower, federal district court for another round of hearings.

On the day of the verdict, E. Pierce vowed not to give up, telling the Associated Press, "I will continue to fight to uphold my father's estate plan and clear my name." He said, "That is a promise that Ms. Smith and her lawyers can take to the bank."

However, he was never able to keep his promise. Two months after the Supreme Court decision, the wrangling over

J. Howard's money suddenly grew cloudier when his sole heir, and Anna's rival, passed away. E. Pierce Marshall unexpectedly died from a brief and extremely vigorous infection.

His attorney, David Margulies, submitted a statement: "Mr. Marshall leaves behind a legacy of being, first and foremost, a remarkable husband, father and grandfather, a successful business visionary and a man of unrivaled perseverance and principle." Surprisingly, after he had spent over a decade of his life supposedly fighting for father's legacy, nowhere is it mentioned that he was a good son.

Anna, showing rare restraint, refused to speak to reporters, instead issuing a statement that, "Out of respect for his family's request for privacy, neither my attorneys nor I will be making any comments." It didn't take long for Pierce's widow, Elaine, to announce that she would be just as dedicated as her late husband had been, in efforts to block Anna from receiving any of the inheritance. Anna responded by filing a new lawsuit, this time against Elaine.

CHAPTER 24

TRAGEDY

> *"Indeed, wretched the man whose
> fame makes his misfortunes famous."*
> —LUCIUS ACCIUS TELEPHUS
> (ROMAN TRAGIC POET, 170-86 BC)

Later that same month, Anna made headlines yet again with a stunning announcement: "I'm pregnant." She did not say who the father was. In September, a pair of events like something out of the soap opera, *Dynasty*, took place. Anna flew to Nassau, the Bahamas, where she gave birth to a six-pound, nine-ounce baby girl she named Dannielynn, satisfying a lifelong dream of having a daughter.

Three days later, on September 10, her twenty-year-old son, Daniel, fell asleep in a chair in her room at Doctors Hospital. When Anna tried to wake him, she couldn't. Almost simultaneously, Anna had gained a daughter and lost her adored son.

The one question on everybody's mind was how on earth did her son die in the hospital room when both Anna and her lawyer were sleeping in that very room? While the toxicology report was pending, there was much speculation as to what had happened. Due to the suddenness of his death at such a young age, the Coroner's Office called the death "suspicious." Until they had exhausted all the possibilities, they could not rule out homicide or suicide, and Anna Nicole's conduct was under suspicion.

The only information that was immediately revealed to the public was that at the time of his death, Daniel was on anti-depressants. No mention was made as to why he was suffering from depression or what it was that ultimately killed him. Daniel had been abusing alcohol and prescription drugs for several years. Anna, who had always been in denial about her own addictive behavior, turned a blind eye. More than that, she understood how her own career would be damaged in the inevitable volcano of media blame if word about Daniel's problem became public knowledge. So, rather than pack him off to a rehab clinic or Alcoholics Anonymous meetings, she watched the son she truly loved sink in an ocean of self-destruction.

Any other mother who ignored a child's self-destructive behavior that way would have had the youngster taken away and made a ward of court; Child Services failed to act because of Anna's celebrity status. Daniel's death wasn't just Anna's fault; it was also society's fault. The authorities too often look the other way when a famous person breaks the law. Sometimes favoritism is no favor—in this case it killed a boy.

The autopsy and toxicology results were expected within the week following his death but they were kept confidential until the date of the Coroner's Inquest. The investigation was supposed to take place on October 23, at which time the case would be presented to a seventeen-member panel that would look into whether Daniel died from overdosing on a prescription drug or whether he had intentionally tried to take his life. Anna Nicole and other witnesses would have been expected to give statements but the Inquest never took place during her lifetime.

The tragedy was under such public scrutiny that CNN felt it deserved to be broadcast nationally and made it their news show's main feature. Daniel K. Stern was a guest on *Larry King Live* on September 26, two weeks after Daniel died. I was asked to appear on the show that evening, but it was too difficult for me to appear on a national show as I was still grieving over Daniel. I also did not feel like I should be on the show out of respect to my nephew and because I was not there when he died and did not know the facts.

No one knows exactly what happened that night. Anna had to be sedated and could barely remember the events herself. Howard K. Stern was there and summarized his side of the story for the world:

He said that Daniel was on an antidepressant called Lexapro. At the time of the interview, the toxicology reports were still pending so that was the only definite substance known to be in his body. Howard admitted that not long before that last visit to his mother, Daniel had to be taken to the hospital. "He went there because he had severe back pains and depression. So he was hospitalized for approximately a week, I think. And, again, it was for depression." He blamed Daniel's unhappy state of mind on a break-up with a girl and said that it had "manifested in his back."

Anna gave birth on September 7, 2006. Daniel arrived in the Bahamas on the night of the ninth. He was going to live with Anna in the Bahamas and go to school there. Howard claims that Anna was "really his [Daniel's] only family." Hello! Of course Daniel has more family—after all, he lived with his grandmother for the first few years of his life. Who does Howard think Virgie and the rest of us are, if not Daniel's family?

Howard goes on to say, "We drove from the airport to the hospital and when we got there, you know, he saw his mom and he hugged his mom and he picked up his baby sister like he'd been around babies his whole life…."

Howard says he was in the room when Daniel passed away, "I was going to sleep on the floor in between the two beds. There were two hospital beds and Anna was in the bed closest to the window and Daniel was in the bed closest to the door. And, Daniel at some point said to me that, you know, he wasn't really that tired, so why didn't I just take the bed and he was going to sit up and watch TV.

"And, remember that Anna had had a C-section two days before, so she needed help and still needs help to get to the bathroom and things like that and Daniel, you know, helped her out to the bathroom and this happened many times throughout the night....

"The next thing that I remember that happened from my perspective is that in the morning Anna said, 'Howard, Howard, Daniel's not breathing.' So I, you know, went over there really quickly. And, at this point Daniel had moved into bed with his mom, so they were actually staying in the same bed. And, I checked Daniel's neck and I didn't feel anything and we called, you know, the nurses and said it was an emergency. And then, medical staff just came rushing into the room and they tried to revive him and they tried to ask or tell Anna and myself to leave but she wasn't going to leave her baby. And she, she stayed there and we were at the foot of the bed and she was hugging Daniel's leg and she was praying to Jesus and she was telling Jesus to take her and not take Daniel....

"When I felt his neck there wasn't a pulse and, you know, we just even after the hospital personnel tried to resuscitate Daniel we, Anna told me to, you know, there was an airbag that they were putting air in and she had me doing that and she was pumping on his chest.

"...Just when they...stopped, Anna screamed out 'No, no!' And she just didn't want to believe that he had died and she didn't want, you know, she wanted to keep trying to save him and keep going. And she had me, you know, pumping the air into his mouth or down his throat and she was pushing on his chest trying to revive him."

They had to sedate Anna at this point because, "she refused to leave her son.... And, you know, the doctors advised us that we should probably check her out of the hospital because the media was going to be coming and it was going to...make the whole situation even worse. So, she did have to be sedated in order to leave."

As well as an autopsy commissioned by Bahamian officials, Anna commissioned a private autopsy. When the toxicology results finally came back, both sources indicated that Daniel had died from the mixture of three prescription drugs, if not more.

The private autopsy was carried out by an American forensic pathologist, Dr. Cyril Wecht. He confirmed with *People* magazine that Daniel's death was caused by a lethal combination of methadone, Zoloft and Lexapro. He also claimed that he knew of four other substances in the boy's body, which included Benadryl, an antihistamine; pseudoephedrine, a decongestant; and a small amount of Ambien, a prescription sleeping pill. However, he said that the latter four drugs were over-the-counter medications and were not "of a potentially lethal nature."

Wecht said that the three primary drugs caused the cardiac dysrhythmia that led to Daniel's death. He put an end to the suggestion that Daniel intentionally killed himself in his statement: "In my opinion it's an accidental death." He said that because Daniel was taking three drugs and not a large dose of a single drug, paired with the fact that he was celebrating a happy occasion with his mother, were factors that pointed to a "tragic accidental drug death."

Asked why Daniel may have been taking methadone, which is sometimes used to help heroin and morphine addicts curb their cravings, Wecht said the drug is "a legitimate prescription drug for pain relief" and that Daniel had "no known history of morphine addiction."

Wecht was not sure if Daniel had a prescription for methadone or for the antidepressant, Zoloft, but it was known that he had been prescribed the other antidepressant Lexapro.

Vickie had hired Wecht to perform a second autopsy in order to put an end to the speculation as to the cause of her son's death. Although the Royal Bahamas Police Force confirmed that they had come to the same conclusion as the private investigator, given Wecht's history, Vickie's choice of coroner was a great cause for suspicion.

The key witness, Dr. Cyril Wecht, has performed over fourteen thousand autopsies, many of which have involved him in high-profile crime cases. He has been involved in investigating the deaths of: Jon Benét Ramsey, claiming that she was not murdered but died accidentally; Elvis Presley, believing that the autopsy performed was a fraud; John F. Kennedy, asserting that he was not shot by a single gunman; and Robert F. Kennedy, claiming he was not murdered by Sirhan Sirhan. Wecht has also controversially suggested that the body of Mary Jo Kopechne should be exhumed for reexamination.

As if his association with these landmark names were not enough to put him in the center of media frenzy, in January 2006, Wecht was indicted by the grand jury on eighty-four counts, ranging from mail fraud and wire fraud to theft. He hired the prestigious former US attorney, Richard Thornburgh, to lead his defense team, and he is going to need all the help he can get. There was one allegation that Wecht stole unclaimed cadavers from the Allegheny County Coroner's Office and sold them while he was Deputy Coroner there. He has also been accused and charged of depositing the Coroner's Office fees into his own account during the same term of office.

Vickie privately hired a corrupt man to lay her son's cause of death to rest, just one more act that has spun this whole situation into an even bigger circus—with Vickie as its ringmaster.

It was not until eleven days after Daniel's death that the authorities issued his death certificate. However, at that time the cause of death was still unknown and the papers stated, "pending chemical analysis." Even after his body was released, the funeral arrangements were delayed for much longer than normal, for no apparent reason. No one including myself could understand why Vickie would not bury her son.

It's so sad that the same thing would happen to Vickie just a few months later when her entire family and her friends could not agree where she should be buried. The fight over her burial continued with courts in two states and orders that prevented Anna from being laid to rest for far too long. I find it so sad that, even after battling through life for thirty-nine years, she could not immediately be laid to rest.

Virgie, Daniel's grandmother, was interviewed on CNN's *Nancy Grace*. When asked why his embalmed body was still sitting in a funeral home, she voiced my feelings, "That's my question, why? That's the last bit of respect that anybody gets in the world, is to be buried. So why is my baby laying in a cold room somewhere and not being buried?"

The funeral had already been delayed because of the inquiry but when the authorities sympathized and issued a death certificate, the cause of Daniel's death continued to be dragged out. Was it for publicity? Maybe it was so that Anna could prepare for the exclusive deals she was going to make with the media. After all, she ended up selling the last pictures taken of Daniel for vast sums of money, apparently to pay for the funeral expenses. She made at least $650,000, and probably quite a bit more. Is this meant to have all gone towards the coffin?

When Howard K. Stern was asked how this money was going to be used, his story conflicted with Anna's. He said that it would be donated to a charity and that the specific organization had not yet been chosen because it would be determined by Daniel's cause of death. Can you really imagine that one cent went towards charity? Which charity would they have chosen? One dedicated to the malpractice of prescription drugs or parental guidance?

SCHEDULE

(Rule) 3

FORM E

(Rule 3A)

Coroner Mrs: Linda R Virgill

COMMONWEALTH OF THE BAHAMAS - MEDICAL CERTIFICATE OF DEATH/STILL BIRTH

Deceased-Name: Surname First Middle Smith Daniel Wayne 1	Sex: M 2	Date and hour of death: Day Month Year Hour 10 9 2006 3 (a)	Date and Birth: Day Month Year 22 1 1986 3 (b) 4	Age at last Birthday 20yrs 5 (a)	Under 1 year: Month days 5 (b)	Under 1 day: Hours Mins. 5 (c)

CAUSE OF DEATH:

Part I

Approximate interval between onset and death

Disease or condition directly leading to death.(a)   Reserved

due to or as a consequence of

Antecedent causes: Pending chemical analysis and Histopathology report.
Morbid conditions, if any, giving rise to the above (b)

due to or as a consequence of

cause, stating the underlying condition last: (c)

6 (i)

Part II

Other significant conditions contributing to the death
but not related to the disease or condition causing it:

6 (ii)

Accident or Injury (Brief description) 7	Autopsy: (yes or no) Yes 8	Case referred to Coroner (yes or no) Yes 9

Certifier's Signature: To the best of my knowledge and belief, death occurred at the time and date and due to the cause(s) stated. Signature: Date: 17/9/2006 10 (a)	Name, qualification and address of certifier: Dr. Govinda Raju & Dr Cyril H. Wecht Pathology Department Princess Margaret Hospital 10 (b)	Name and address of attending physician if other than certifier: 10 (c)

Confirmation of cause of death in case of cremation:
I have examined the dead body and hereby confirm the cause of death as certified above.

Signature: Date: 11 (a)	Name and address of medical practitioner confirming cause: 11 (b)

Place of death: (Specify hospital or address of other place) Doctor's Hospital 12 (a)	If hospital, indicate: inpatient/ op/Emergency Room /DOA 12 (b)	Usual Residence, address and island 13	Citizen: (Name of Country) USA 14	Occupation 15

Married, never married Widowed, Divorced, (specify) 16	Spouse-Name: (if wife, give maiden name) Surname First Middle 17	Survived by Spouse & (yes o no) 18	Father's Name: Surname First Middle 19	Mothers Maiden Name: Surname First Middle 20

Informant's Signature: I certify that the above particulars are true to the best of my knowledge and belief. Signature: Date: 21 (a)	Informant's relation to deceased or other description: 21 (b)	Name and address of Informant: 21 (c)

Disposition: (Person to whom body is released) Signature: Date: Name and Address: 22 (a)	Type of disposition:(specify burial, cremation, removal, etc) 22 (b)	Date of Disposition: Date Month Year 22 (c)	Name and location of cemetery, crematory or other place of disposition: 22 (d)

Apparently, seven times the prescribed amount of anti-depressants were found in Daniel's bloodstream. The question that should be asked is, who was responsible? Just as Nancy Grace pointed out, "Somebody had to give it to him. He had to get it from somewhere." Was his doctor so irresponsible that he gave him that much in his prescription, or did he get it from elsewhere? And where did his addiction stem from in the first place: his girlfriend, his back pain, or his upbringing?

Virgie did not hesitate before throwing out accusations. She said to *In Touch Weekly* that, "It was murder, I know it was, and someone has to pay." She was adamant that Daniel "did not overdose himself" and, if it wasn't suicide, then only her daughter, Anna Nicole, and Howard K. Stern are left to blame. I don't think that her accusations were entirely directed at Anna. I think Anna may have been indirectly responsible for her son's death but I definitely don't think that she would intentionally let her son die. He was her life-support. However, there are a lot of questions about the turn of events that remain unanswered.

Nancy Grace asked Virgie, as a police officer of twenty-eight years, what she found unusual. She responded, "that he died in a hospital, to start with, people coming in and out, and that there were two other people in that room with him. Somebody should have noticed something…he slept through the whole thing? When you overdose, usually you have some sort of convulsion. It just depends. …[H]ow long ago was it that Daniel was tested at the normal hospital where he went to have check-ups? Was his blood tested there? …[D]id he show anything in his blood there?"

There are so many holes in the story that it is no wonder issues have been raised and still haven't been answered. When Anna failed to defend herself against the allegations being made against her, people filled in the blanks for themselves.

Virgie is Daniel's grandmother and yet, like the rest of us, she knows nothing about his death because she wasn't there and

Anna had stopped her son from seeing Virgie for years. Virgie told Nancy Grace, "[A]s far as I know, he was never on anything. And if he wanted to be, in his teenage years, he could have—he had a whole assortment of drugs he could have gotten from his mother…" However, Virgie obviously didn't know anything about Daniel's later life because he was on a whole assortment of prescription drugs for years and she knew nothing about it.

Virgie told Nancy Grace that the only time she had spoken to her daughter in years was when Anna called right after Daniel had died and tried to tell her what had happened. "She called but you couldn't understand anything she said because you could tell she was clearly under some kind of—of drug because she was very upset. She was mumbling like a drunk does. You know, all I got out of it was that Daniel's dead. And then it—you know, it was like she was in the middle of a sentence and the phone hung up. And that's all I got to hear from her." Virgie wasn't able to contact her daughter again because Anna changed her number after she called. Therefore, Virgie's speculations were just as presumptuous as everyone else's. Only Howard and Anna would ever know what happened in the hospital room on the night of September 10, 2006.

At the same time Virgie released her interview, *Entertainment Tonight* asked me to tell my side of the story and what I thought about the circumstances around Daniel's death. Again, I refused to go public, not only out of respect for Daniel, but also because I knew that it would piss Anna off. At the end of the interview, Virgie offered her support to Anna through a TV screen, but she knew that by making a public statement about Daniel's death she would infuriate Anna. Virgie did it anyway and Anna denounced her as a mother. They never spoke again.

Before Daniel's death, he had mostly been kept on the sidelines of Anna's very public life. He was most famous for having his photo taken with Anna and as a teenage boy growing up on the *Anna Nicole Smith Show*. He would rarely say a word if the camera was rolling and seemed generally embarrassed when his crazed mother forced him to kiss her on the cheek in front of most of America's TV-watching audience.

Following his death, the media tried to dig into his background and dish out anything they could find. For the first time, Daniel was in the center spotlight and the public was able to find out who he was and, whether or not he was ever happy being parented by Anna. The *Los Angeles Times* wrote: "So much has been written about the death of twenty-year-old Daniel Wayne Smith but so little is known of the young man himself."

In the meantime, his death has been picked over in every publication from *Star* magazine to the *Hindustan Times*: Who was the third person in the hospital room? Was the death from natural or unnatural causes? Was it his heart or the antidepressants he took or an overdose of something else? And how could his mother have sold photos of him to *In Touch* for $400,000 less than twenty-four hours after his death?

CHAPTER 25

DANIEL WAYNE SMITH

*W*ho was Daniel and what was his all too short life like? He was always very camera shy and so the only glimpse we ever had was of him hiding behind his mother. Despite Anna's efforts to turn him into a star, Daniel wanted to blend into the background, and so, even after his death, much of his life remains anonymous.

Daniel Wayne Smith was born on January 22, 1986, in Limestone, Texas. His mother was eighteen at the time. She was working at Jim's Krispy Fried Chicken and had married his father, a cook at the restaurant, one year before. She said that her husband, Billy Smith, was nice to her while they were dating but once they got married he was abusive and jealous. He would get angry every time she wanted to go out and she thought that by having a baby all their problems would go away. She said, "Well, if I was to have a baby, I would never be lonely." However, nothing helped to save her marriage and it ended in a messy divorce one year later.

Virgie Arthur, Anna Nicole's estranged mother, claims she brought up Daniel for the first six years of his life while his mother looked for work (which she found stripping in Dallas). It wasn't until Anna Nicole found success as a model that she brought Daniel to live with her and cut off communication with her mother. Anna contradicted this with her story that she only let Daniel live with Virgie for a couple of years before getting him back—then again, she also admitted she was never good with dates.

Our brother, Donnie often stayed at Anna's ranch in Tomball. He hung out with Daniel more than he did with Vickie. They had a lot of fun together and grew really close. Anna gave them tickets to go to the premiere of *Aladdin* and so Donnie took his nephew. They played videogames and went to arcades. Anna loved to be chauffeured around in a limo and always had one on tap so, even when she wasn't around, Daniel and Donnie traveled in style.

Our father, Donald, gave *Extra* a videotape of when Anna first reunited with her father and brother in Los Angeles. It shows Donnie around the same age that Daniel was when he died. Even Donnie admits the resemblance is uncanny. (The video belonged to Donnie and is one of the many possessions I believe our father stole from him.)

Anna loved Daniel and would always make sure he was cared for. He had a string of nannies, one of whom was Maria Cerrato, the housekeeper who sued Anna for sexual abuse. He was also looked after by a man called Nassir Samirami, apparently one of the only men Anna hired and did not have an affair with. Sam was like a parent to Daniel. He took the boy to and from school, fed him, dressed him, and made sure he was having a good time.

Anna tried her best to be a mother to Daniel, buying him toys, and giving him spurts of undivided attention, but she also treated him like a doll, making him pierce his ears and grow his hair long, so that he looked like a girl. She was also very spontaneous and did not provide Daniel with a stable upbringing. Virgie's sister, Kay Beal, was quoted as saying that "Anna pulls away from everybody that gets close to Daniel. If you show him too much love and kindness, she thinks you want something for it." She therefore did not let anybody, other than herself, get close to Daniel, and eventually refused to let him speak to any members of the family he had once grown attached to.

Daniel spent his school years in a series of different private schools. He also had small parts in some of his mother's films playing a ring bearer in 1995's *To the Limit* and Billy Ray in *Skyscraper*. Donnie says that Daniel wanted to be a movie star when he was really young but I think that ambition quickly faded.

When Daniel was sixteen his mother became the star of her own reality television show called *The Anna Nicole Show* and he was (not surprisingly) a recurring character. The makeup artist on the show remembers him as a shy, sweet kid, and that Anna Nicole was often worried that the camera crews were upsetting him. The blurb about him on the show's website describes him as a "straight-A student" and "sweet, quiet and shy."

It was reported that Daniel attended classes at Valley College in the summer of 2006, including all the introductory basics—economics, anthropology, math, philosophy and English. "I didn't know him," said student Christina Corigliano, who was interviewed by *Entertainment Tonight*. "But I saw him a few times going to class and I thought he was cute." It has also been reported that Daniel was taking antidepressants for depression over a girl.

Gabriel Rotello, the producer of VH1's unauthorized documentary, *Dark Roots*, wrote a blog about Anna and I guess you can say this was his tribute to Daniel and Vickie:

"[O]ne thing always struck me about Anna Nicole Smith while I interviewed her friends and family for that film [*Dark Roots*].

"Despite the huge number of bitter enemies she had made—including discarded childhood friends, discarded family members, discarded former lovers, and the family of her deceased millionaire husband—virtually all of them reluctantly admitted one undeniable fact: Anna Nicole was a deeply devoted mother who passionately loved her son Daniel, lived for him, sacrificed for him, and placed him at the center of her life.

"Most of Anna's critics also reluctantly agreed that despite his mother's chaotic life, Daniel had turned out surprisingly well: Then 17, he was a normal student and avid high school athlete who seemed genuinely well adjusted, even serious, and who was, in turn, devoted to his mother.

"I was certainly no fan of the mother, but I was saddened by the death of the son this week. And I'm equally saddened to watch the media use his death to take cheap shots.

"According to reports, Anna kept trying to resuscitate Daniel after medical workers gave up. Reports also say that she had to be heavily sedated afterwards, and was disoriented when she awoke.

"Both reports seem understandable for a parent who had just given birth and who then witnessed the unexpected death of a 20-year-old child.

"But these reports have been twisted, predictably, into lurid headlines—even on this blog—of an Anna Nicole who was so 'drugged' she 'forgot' her son had died. The implication being, it was just one more wild weekend for that whacky freak, Anna Nicole.

"The temptation to snicker is apparently overwhelming. But it should be resisted. Daniel's death, whatever its cause, must be unbearable for his mother. To use it as a means to poke fun says more about the mockers than the mocked.

"Don't get me wrong: Media hounds like Anna deserve all the scrutiny they invite. And the mystery of Daniel's death makes it a legitimate subject of media attention.

"But attention is one thing, snickering is something else. No grieving mom deserves that. Even if her name is Anna Nicole Smith."

One response from Rotello's readers was:

"This dreadful quirk of fate is even sadder than it is weird.

The fact that it happened to a real live cartoon character doesn't make it any less tragic.

"There is something horribly voyeuristic in breathing down a mother's neck at a tragedy. And some things are just best left unexamined in the press.

"No matter how extreme this woman's actions, she doesn't deserve to be treated so cruelly. Would you trade places for all the money or beauty or fame in the world if it meant having to pay that price with your children?"

On October 7, 2006, Daniel's father's side of the family held a memorial service for him. Even though his funeral had not yet taken place, his father, Billy, and other family members wanted to mourn their loss. Daniel's death had been in the papers every day since it had happened and Billy's family probably felt that they needed to have some kind of response.

The memorial service took place in Mexia at the First Baptist Church. Apparently over seventy friends and family members attended. Billy called the media and invited them to write about the service but, without Daniel's body or Anna, their interest waned.

Billy invited Elaine, Virgie, me and all of Daniel's cousins. Although they all showed up, I wanted to pay my respects privately and considered the Mexia memorial service to be a charade I did not want to participate in. After many of those who attended told me about the service, I am even more certain I made the right choice.

Billy had never been much of a father to Daniel so it was a bit weird that he organized a separate funeral service for his son. He had never made any effort to bring up Daniel and neither had his family. Billy only contacted Daniel once Anna had made a name for herself and even then he didn't make much of an effort. He called a few times but Billy didn't want custody over his son, he just wanted some of the media attention.

On Thursday, October 19, thirty-six days after Daniel's death, Anna held the funeral for him. For all of us back in Texas, it was really sad that we could not attend the service in the Bahamas, even more so because Anna invited twenty-five people but no members of her family. Daniel was buried at the Lakeview Memorial Gardens in his trucker cap, blue jeans and a T-shirt—his favorite clothes.

No one was allowed to communicate with Daniel towards the end of his life. Anna always shut out everyone that got close to him. I can see why she wanted to cut her family off. In her mind, if we were not around she would be able to pretend that she was better than us and above her Texas roots. But to isolate Daniel from everybody he grew close to was upsetting for everyone who knew him, especially his family.

When Vickie sold the last photos taken of Daniel and the pictures of his funeral and then married Howard before her son was buried, I was asked to respond to my sister's actions. I told the media that I could not understand why she had done these things. She was Daniel's mother. It broke my heart that she exploited his death like that.

I was quoted by the tabloids as saying, "[Anna] waits forever to bury him and two days after he dies, she's selling pictures of him to the tabloids and I'm thinking, 'What a freaking waste of a human being, my sister is.'" I would never say that, no matter what our differences are; the journalists just wrote what they wanted to hear. I would never say that about any family member and I was really hurt that they would write that when I couldn't defend myself. I did not want her to read something so hurtful with all she was going through.

I did not want to condemn my sister because I did not know what she was going through. I was upset by the way Daniel's death and funeral service were orchestrated. My children and I were in tears when Daniel died; he was family, our blood, and we loved him. He was too young to die.

Anna and I had a cousin, Mickey Jean. He was Donald's sister, Linda's, son. Mickey too died tragically. He was eighteen years old when his car crashed into a tree. He was still breathing when the firemen pried his vehicle open with the Jaws of Life, but he died within minutes. They found high levels of alcohol and drugs in his blood stream.

Linda had two children with her husband, Michael. Just like Billy Smith, he was never around for them. He went to his son's funeral, but even the tragedy of his son's death didn't make him a better father for his daughter, Brandy.

Linda is my father's only sibling. She is blonde and attractive. She was a really young mother; she had Mickey Jean when she was seventeen and her daughter, Brandy, four years later. She always tried to be a cool mom by letting her children drink and smoke weed around her. Linda and her son had a really close relationship and they looked after each other like Daniel and Anna.

Mickey was very depressed though and started drinking excessively and taking drugs. His mother always dated people much younger than her and it took its toll on him. She would get drunk and embarrass him by being sexually open in his presence and he felt uncomfortable around her.

The night he crashed, he had found his mother and a childhood friend of his making out. His friend was only eighteen, the same age as him and he ran away to escape. He was way over the limit and stoned, too, so he was in no condition to drive but he didn't care.

After Mickey Jean died, Linda stopped seeing his friend. She took it really badly and sank into depression. For years, she kept his room exactly as it was when he lived in it and no one was allowed to touch a thing. Brandy blamed her mother for her Mickey's death and often publicly lashed out at her. She said it was her mother's fault for letting him drink and for embarrassing him in front of his friends. At Mickey Jean's funeral, Linda let his friends place joints in her son's casket in memory of him. I thought that was really disturbing, considering the fact that that is what had killed him.

The tragedy of Mickey's death had a dramatic effect on our family. Linda and her mother, Helen, owned and ran a liquor store, but after the crash, she sold it and the whole family stopped drinking. Even my father changed his attitude a lot and, although he will never quit smoking marijuana, he stopped drinking alcohol.

Mickey made the whole family completely change its ways and I hoped that Daniel's death would make Anna realize she had to be more responsible, especially with the birth of her baby daughter. Unfortunately, I think it had the reverse effect on Anna. Ultimately, she lived for only five months after losing her beloved son.

BAHAMA MAMA
DRAMA

"Whose your daddy?"
—THE NATIONAL LEDGER

On September 15, 2006, Getty Images sent out a mass e-mail to every existing celebrity-hungry publication, offering them the exclusive rights to photos taken of Anna Nicole Smith in the hospital with her son, Daniel, and newborn daughter. These seventeen photos were the last pictures taken of Daniel before he died and the only record of the three family members together. A bidding war ensued for the last photos of Daniel and *In Touch Weekly* ended up forking out $400,000 for the exclusive print rights, while *Entertainment Tonight* and *The Insider* succumbed to a fee of at least $250,000 for the television rights.

Where did Getty Images get these photos from and who ended up cashing in? Anna Nicole, of course. She exploited her son's death and the birth of her daughter, squeezing every last penny that she could out of the tragedy, and what should have been a very private mourning process.

On November 6, 2006, the whole world was invited to see the birth of Anna's baby daughter, Dannielynn Hope Smith. She sold the video recording of her C-section to *Entertainment Tonight* for $1 million, which aired exactly two months after she had given birth. The uncensored video left absolutely nothing to the imagination. It showed Anna lying back, half-sedated, while the doctor used a metal clamp to pull the baby out of her sliced-open stomach. She had an epidural, even though she says she felt everything and was in a lot of pain. The entire time, Anna repeatedly groaned, "I wanna see my baby," despite the fact that it had not yet left her womb.

This was how photographer, Larry Birkhead, witnessed the birth of his alleged daughter. Just as the hype over Daniel's death was subsiding, the headlines once again flashed Anna Nicole Smith's name, this time questioning who the father of her child was. Larry Birkhead had announced to the world that he was the baby's father on *Entertainment Tonight*, to a very responsive media. He was not the only man to claim to be Dannielynn's father. Following Larry's lead, two more men came forward. Five months later, after Anna died, almost an entire phone book of men came out of the woodwork, including at least one millionaire, a prince, an immigration officer, and a bodyguard. Most of the pretenders were willing to take a DNA test to prove that he was the father and to stay in the media.

The National Ledger's article began: "The phrase whose your daddy is taking on a whole new meaning for Anna Nicole's baby girl, Dannielynn Hope, the daughter of Anna Nicole Smith. According to a release from TrimSpa, more daddies have line[d] up for baby Smith's fifteen Minutes of Fame."

"TrimSpa's first media inquiry regarding the 'new prospects' was thought to be a bad joke, but the topic resurfaced throughout the day in multiple media outlets. 'By day's end,' said a company representative, 'we were prepared to hear that every eligible bachelor was stepping up for the job.'"

To put all the rumors to rest, Howard K. Stern declared on *Larry King Live* that he was the father of Anna's daughter. Sorry, that he was the "proud father"—this he repeated three times. He told Larry King that he and Anna had been very much in love for a while but had kept it a secret. He said that there was no need for a DNA test because, "based on the timing of when the baby was born there really is no doubt."

Howard denied that Larry was ever Anna's boyfriend and, when asked if their relationship had been intimate, he avoided the question, saying that being so close to Daniel's death it was inappropriate to discuss the subject matter.

Four months later, Larry Birkhead was invited on the same show. According to him Howard K. Stern's answers were just "one big lie." He told Larry King that he and Anna had met at The Barnstable Brown Kentucky Derby party and they had been dating for two-and-a-half years. They had been trying to have a baby for a while but she had had a miscarriage before conceiving their daughter. When asked why he and Anna had split up, he blamed Howard K. Stern for interfering with their relationship and causing tension between them.

Howard was jealous of Larry because he wanted Anna for himself. According to Birkhead, not only was Anna not physically interested in Howard, at times she also had to force him out of her life. "Most of the time that—that I was in the home with her, when we lived together, we would have to basically lock doors to the bedroom. He would try to come in and she'd have to tell him at certain points to call before he came back."

"…One time in particular, while she was pregnant, I had to basically rescue her at a hotel because Howard gave her so much grief about me being the father and saying that he was never going to accept me. And he told her to make a choice…him or me. And she called me crying hysterical and she drove herself barefoot to a hotel down the street and I had to basically help her."

To say that Larry Birkhead and Anna were never a couple is obviously a lie because there are too many intimate photos of them together to prove otherwise. There are so many factors that make Howard K. Stern seem incredible as both Anna's lover and as Dannielynn's father. For a start, it was very suspicious that Howard and Anna kept their sexual relationship a secret for over a year and only decided to

Certificate no. 14598

BIRTHS REGISTRATION
CERTIFIED COPY OF ENTRY IN REGISTER OF BIRTHS

Occupation of Mother: ACTRESS   Marital Status: Widow   Age: 38
Occupation of Father: Attorney   Age: 37

Where Mother Born:	United States	Where Father Born:	United States

Birth: Single   Total No. of Children Born to Mother
(Single, Twin, Triplet, or Other)   (1) Alive - (including this birth):   2
                                     (2) No. Living at date of this birth: 1

Permanent Residence at HORIZONS   Bahamas
time of birth   EASTERN ROAD   New Providence
                                          Eastern District

Certificate no. 14598

BIRTHS REGISTRATION
CERTIFIED COPY OF ENTRY IN REGISTER OF BIRTHS

Child's Surname: STERN
Child's Christian
or First Names: DANNIELYNN   HOPE MARSHALL

Sex: Female   Date of Birth: 7th September 2006 admit it once the identity of her baby's father was in question. There are people who witnessed Anna and Larry Birkhead's affair, during the time that Howard says *he* was with Anna. There is also a witness who testified Anna would never have thought of Howard K. Stern sexually and that she was even repulsed by the idea.

Larry Birkhead insisted that he was the father and that he was willing to take a paternity test to prove it. Why then would Anna not have had a DNA test to end yet another futile court battle? Larry Birkhead incurred $300,000 worth of attorney's fees trying to make Anna agree to a paternity test. In October he had to turn to the courts to make Anna come back from the Bahamas and take a paternity and drug test. (He fears that his daughter's health may be in danger because her mother took drugs during her pregnancy.) The procedure is cheap and easy to do; they swipe the inside of the mouth with a Q-tip and it's over in less than sixty seconds. If Howard K. Stern was the real father then why not reveal the truth once and for all and put Larry Birkhead out of his misery?

January 23, 2007 was the last day Anna had to submit to a DNA paternity test, but there was no way Anna would be coerced into anything. By staying in the Bahamas she could be above the law and any court rulings.

The only obstacle she had to get past was the fact that the government of the Bahamas only permits citizenships under the following guidelines: that you are an investor/owner of a business, or you own a home that is valued over $500,000. Since Anna did not purchase her former boyfriend's Bahamian home that she was occupying, she was not considered a citizen and could, therefore, be deported. She was rumored to say if that happened she would have Daniel's body exhumed and taken back with her to Los Angeles. It took thirty-nine days for her to bury the young man, to exhume him would be crazy.

By this point she had lost her claim that G. Ben Thompson's mansion was a gift to her. She was ordered to vacate the premises known as "Horizons" on the Eastern Road, New Providence and was forced to move into a much more modest home. She didn't care. There was no way she was going to go back to America to face the wrath of Larry Birkhead and his legal team.

Instead of putting an end to everybody's suspicions, Anna sent an AOL instant message to her ex the night before the DNA was due and told him that she would not comply with his demands.

Anna Nicole: quit trash me at the casino

Larry: not at a casino

Anna Nicole: go f**k my mom to

Anna Nicole: Yall are sick

Larry: show up for the test with the baby

Anna Nicole: don't think so

Anna Nicole: u wish

Larry: everybody just want u to do right thing is all

Anna Nicole: in your dreams

As well as attracting a lot of media attention to herself, Anna obviously had a reason for wanting us to believe that Howard K. Stern was the father of her child. To further increase our suspicions, Howard was not even Anna's first choice. Before Howard's appearance on *Larry King Live*, Anna had insisted that her other ex-lover, G. Ben Thompson, was the father, but this was invalidated when he informed the media that he could not even qualify as a candidate. He had had a vasectomy.

This did not stop Anna from living in his house though. He was a real estate developer and when she told him she wanted to move to the Bahamas to get away from the media, he found her a house there. Then when the time came for her to pay up, she refused to sign for the mortgage. She claimed that she didn't have to pay for the house because G. Ben Thompson had promised it to her as a gift. Just like every other house in Anna's life, she expected to live in this million-dollar property for free.

G. Ben Thompson was not having it though. Why should he pay for Anna and her attorney to live on his property, when he did not even want the house in the first place? At first, he felt sorry for Anna because she was pregnant and not well, but once she got better, he turned to the courts to get her evicted. While the court order was being processed, Anna and Howard stayed put. At one point they remained in the house with no electricity as Thompson had contacted the power company to pull the plug.

On October 30, 2006, Anna gave *Entertainment Tonight* her first televised interview since her son's death. Anna explained how she was a prisoner, trapped in her million-dollar estate—that she had yet to pay for. She was to be evicted on October 31, 2006, but instead that day she admitted herself into a Bahamas hospital with claims of pneumonia. Mark Steines from ET had just come back from interviewing her in the Bahamas. On camera, she looked tanned and healthy; vibrant from the birth of her daughter; and then, within a week, she was in the hospital with a collapsed lung.

CHAPTER 27

THE COMMITMENT CEREMONY

> *"Be very careful about who
> you hang around with,
> because you may be next."*
> —VIRGIE ARTHUR ON NANCY GRACE

When Larry King asked Howard K. Stern if marriage between he and Anna would be sooner rather than later, Stern's answer was: "Well, it probably would have been sooner, you know, but for Daniel's death and I just think we have to get through—we really haven't been allowed to grieve with the way that this whole thing has been handled. And, you know, I—it's going to be I think a little while before, you know, we're going to be able to experience real happy moments."

Contrary to this, they got "married" on September 28, just two days later. Under three weeks after Vickie's son died, she married Howard K. Stern on a catamaran in Nassau, Bahamas.

No wait! The couple had a commitment ceremony and exchanged vows. Although it was not formally a wedding, Anna wore a white tulle wedding dress and veil and Stern changed into a dark suit for the occasion. After a few mimosas the couple jumped into the ocean fully clothed, with cameras flashing like crazy from the shore.

Yet again, Anna had an occasion to sell exclusive photos of herself and her family for a fortune: *People* magazine paid her $1 million for them. Anything for attention, that was Vickie's way. She would always say: "Any publicity is good publicity." She just wanted people to talk about her. She wanted her name in the headlines and, with no end in sight, that is what she got.

Anna had an ability to draw out any scenario so that people kept having to tune in for more. Her life was an addictive soap opera that drip-fed you scandal like scores of heroin. She turned herself into an enigma that everyone wanted to understand, but at what cost? Everybody may want to read about her but, by withholding the truth from the public, she was inviting us to speculate and slander her.

There are so many rumors circulating and, whether or not they are true, they are horrible. Even her own mother came forward and questioned the truth behind her grandson's death. The papers went to the extreme of calling Anna a murderer and a witness was willing to testify that Howard K. Stern gave Daniel the pills that killed him. The witness claimed that Howard gave Daniel methadone and flushed the pills down the toilet after he died. Following that news, a coroner's inquest would take place after all.

The public is even more critical of Howard K. Stern than of Anna. Anna had the excuse that she was like a helpless child, who could not be held accountable for the consequences of her actions. Howard, on the other hand, is being accused of masterminding everything that has gone wrong.

Anna's mother, Virgie, was furious that her daughter exchanged vows with a man she would not trust with a ten-foot pole. She told Nancy Grace: "Howard is out there, and, you know, it seems like he's controlling her life...he doesn't allow us to talk to her. You know, he changed the phone numbers. Nobody in the family is allowed to talk—she has family. She has a lot of family."

In their bitter war, Larry Birkhead's attorney, Debra Opri, found evidence against Howard. It seems from these investigations that he was the person who supplied Anna with drugs; though we need to hear his response. Debra secretly had private investigators follow Anna and Howard while they were in the Bahamas and they found out that Anna had seven aliases. With each of these names, she could collect another dose of prescription drugs so that she had enough to feed her habit. That meant that she was taking seven times the amount of drugs prescribed for one person.

Even while she was pregnant Anna could not give up her addiction. There are photos of her drinking during her pregnancy and Larry Birkhead says that he was upset by the fact that she was still taking drugs while they were building a life for their baby.

While Vickie was busy taking drugs on Planet Anna Nicole, Howard K. Stern could orchestrate her life. Anna's ex-publicist, David Granoff, said that he was no longer allowed to deal directly with Anna once Howard K. Stern came into the picture. Stern, her live-in lawyer mediated everything on her behalf. He made decisions, which he told people had come from Anna, but the truth always comes out eventually. Later it became obvious that Anna never even knew anything was being decided. After going back and forth with Howard K. Stern, acting on Anna's behalf, David got a call from Anna asking him why he was doing this. Anna had no idea what was going on behind her back.

It is plain to see the control that Howard K. Stern had on Vickie and that it was far from healthy. It wasn't a good relationship. I know; I've seen those kinds before. Just recently the famous shock jock, Howard Stern, said he had to (unfortunately) live with the fact that "that guy is running around" with the same name.

On *The Anna Nicole Show*, Howard K. Stern never left her side. In media shots we can always see him lurking in the background. Between them, they cut off Anna's entire family, all her friends, and every man that she had ever been involved with.

Howard finally got his way. After over a decade of friend-ship, he and Anna were finally a couple and his greatest threat, Larry Birkhead, was left in the dark. But how much can we rely on what we are told? After all, Anna and Howard had lied to the public in the past, why should we trust them now?

On June 1, 2006 Anna confirmed for the media that she was pregnant. She had always wanted a daughter and now she would finally have a baby girl. But it was not as she had planned. She did not want to bring up the baby with Larry Birkhead and she certainly did not want to share her long-awaited daughter with him.

As soon as Larry Birkhead came forward and threatened to sue Anna, she needed someone else to claim paternity. That is when Howard K. Stern conveniently stepped in and declared that he was the father, that they were very much in love, and had plans to get married. Just to make sure their decision was final, Dannielynn's birth certificate listed Howard as the father and "Stern" as her last name. Anything to get Birkhead out of the picture.

However, Birkhead was not going to give up without a fight. He had already made it very clear that, whether she liked it or not, he would see to it that a paternity test was taken. His name was plastered across the international tabloids and he gave inter-views to every major American TV show and publication pleading with Anna to take the test. He hired a lawyer and took Anna to court, and filed an individual claim against Howard K. Stern for fraudulently claiming to be his baby's father.

To make matters even worse for Anna, a friend of hers came forward on November 8 and testified that Larry Birkhead *was* the father. The testimony was leaked to the press, even though by law it should have been kept confidential. The declaration involves a minor and therefore was supposed to be kept sealed but somehow its entire content was exposed.

According to Anna's friend, Laurie Payne's, sworn statement, Anna thought Stern was disgusting. Laurie spent a lot of time with Anna while she was pregnant and when she asked Anna why she hadn't gotten into a relationship with Stern before, Anna replied, "EWWW...GROSS! No way! I would never!" Anna has been "best friends" with her attorney for twelve years and yet there had been no hint of a sexual relationship between them. Her own son had been quoted as criticizing the attorney for not getting any "p*ssy," despite being around for all these years. The declaration also includes an e-mail Anna sent to Laurie, proving that a lot of the information she gave was true.

DEBRA A. OPRI (State Bar No. 140206)
CPRI & ASSOCIATES
A Professional Law Corporation
9383 Wilshire Boulevard, Suite 830
Los Angeles, California 90211-2407
Tel (323)658-6774
Fax (323)658-5160

Attorney For Petitioner
Larry Birkhead

SUPERIOR COURT OF THE STATE OF CALIFORNIA

FOR THE COUNTY OF LOS ANGELES

| In re Matter of

LARRY BIRKHEAD

Petitioner,

VICKIE LYNN MARSHALL

Respondent | CASE NO. BF 030 239
[Re-assigned to Hon. Robert A. Schnider Dept. 2]

DECLARATION OF LAURIE PAYNE IN SUPPORT OF PETITIONER'S OPPOSITION TO RESPONSDENT'S MOTION TO QUASH AND/OR DISMISS

Date: November 8, 2005
Time: 830 a.
Dept.: 2 |

DECLARATION OF LAURIE PAYNE

I, LAURIE PAYNE, declare and state:

1.   I am an adult individual over 18 years of age. I am not a party to the within action, Birkhead v. Marshall, Los Angeles Superior Court Case No. BF 030239. The following is within my personal knowledge, unless stated otherwise, and if called to so testify, I could and would competently do so.

2.   I am a resident of Myrtle Beach, South Carolina. The Respondent Vickie Lynn Marshall a/k/a Anna Nicole Smith and I first met in approximately July 2005. At that time, I flew down to the Florida Keys to vacation with friends and Respondent spent several days there with our mutual friend, G. Ben Thompson.

3.   The Respondent and I "hit it off" immediately. We both shared a love of dogs and socializing. When Respondent left, we remained in contact by telephone, emails, instant messages. We exchanged pictures of our trip and, in fact, a picture one of the girls took while on vacation was sent to Respondent of her and her late son Daniel on a raft is now prominently placed on her website.

4.   The Respondent, myself and another friend all had birthdays at the end of November, and Respondent stated that she wanted to celebrate our birthdays together as well as celebrate the holidays in Myrtle Beach. Respondent stated it would be nice to be with a big, loving family for the holidays since she didn't have one. Respondent spent a significant amount of time in Myrtle Beach in November and December 2005. I never met the Petitioner, Larry Birkhead. However, during this time Respondent would talk frequently about him. Respondent never claimed a serious relationship with Petitioner, however, I caught her at various times communicating with him by text messaging and cell phone calls after she claimed to me to have changed her phone number to avoid him.

5.   I first learned that the Respondent was pregnant by way of an email she sent to me, a true and correct copy of which is attached hereto as Exhibit "A". In this email, Respondent claimed to have had sex only three times during the conception period, once

1

in December, and two times in January, 2006. Respondent also stated in this email that she was, "high risk again". When I subsequently spoke with Respondent directly by telephone, I asked her why she was considered "high risk", at which time **she admitted to me that she was previously pregnant by Larry Birkhead** but had lost the baby due to a miscarriage.

6.   I have personal knowledge from Respondent herself that Howard K. Stern is not the father of her child, Dannielynn, born September 7, 2006. When Respondent was visiting during Christmas 2005, we were all sitting together in Myrtle Beach, including Howard K. Stern. We all had been drinking and Howard began to tease Respondent's son Daniel about being a 19-year old virgin. Annoyed, Daniel looked at Stern and stated, "I don't know why you're worried about me, you've been around my mother for 12 years and haven't had any p*ssy either". During this same visit, I questioned Respondent regarding the fact that Stern was always hanging around and why it was so hard to visit with her alone. **I asked her why she did not just go into a relationship with Stern, to which Respondent responded, "EWWW... GROSS!!! No way!! I would never!"**

7.   In May, 2006 Respondent specifically informed me during telephone calls as well as via computer "instant messages" that Larry Birkhead was, in fact, the father of her then unborn child Dannielynn. Apparently she and Mr. Birkhead had a "love-hate" relationship and she would refer to Mr. Birkhead as, "the asshole" in our discussions about this fact. The Respondent admitted in an "instant message" that she was sick with flu-like symptoms upon returning home from Myrtle Beach the first of January, 2005, and that Birkhead had come over to her LA home to care for her at which time they had sexual relations on two different occasions.

8.   Respondent again visited Myrtle Beach during May 2006, when she was visibly pregnant with Dannielynn. Respondent stayed at a mutual friend's beach house, and I saw her almost every day that she was visiting. Respondent did not like to do anything for herself, and requested my help in taking what she claimed were her medications that had to be taken around the clock. As a result, at Respondent's direction I personally opened

Respondent's pill bottles and handed her pills and a bottle of water. *I was very curious and concerned as to what "medications" Respondent was taking while pregnant and viewed the label on the pill bottles which indicated Respondent was taking Methadone*. Respondent had pills in 10 mg and 5 mg doses. In addition, I personally observed that Respondent had a different name—not hers—on these methadone pill bottles. *Respondent was also taking other medications during this time while pregnant*, one of which I personally observed to be a rather high dose of Xanax.

I declare under penalty of perjury under the laws of the State of California that the foregoing is true and correct.

Executed this __1__ day of November, 2006 at Myrtle Beach, South Carolina.

Laurie Payne

Laurie Payne,
Declarant

Subj: Re: Ok!!! Now I get worried!!!!!
Date: 5/9/2006 6:53:18 A.M. Eastern Daylight Time
From:
To:

Hey I will be ok I talked to gina ford and ben today they were so nice to me!.......................i wish I lived there I hate it here!...............tired of being alone!.............and now more than ever I cant leave my house press everywhere!!......................just want to be happy and that lil fuck wont leave me alone and treats me like shit in front of his friends it has always been them over me, when hes in Kentucky oh im a bitch and hes so damm mean sends me texts so hateful!....................ive changed all my numbers 3 times got a great security system sohe don't get in without the alarm going off!!!!.................but he got in in jan................when I was very sick do u remember what I told you???.................well one of two people once in dec and twice in jan........................you do the math but I hear someone cant do what has been done!.....................so hear I go again alone and at high risk this time no ones happy for me so how can I be and that's so sad cause its all I ever wanted but not alone!.......................just got out of the hospital and they were worried about me not the other I said don't even go there!...............i finally got out was to scared of what they might do!....................I cant work now so im pretty much fucked for a bit!............sure counting on the court to give me my money fast!.....................cause all I want to do is move from this house and get a better one and just start over!...............and to boot ive gained 30 pounds im horrified!.................but I wanted to be excited but how can I when nobody else is!................i should of took ben up on his offer of getting me a house and someone to take care of me but bad timeing I guess or stupidity!!!!!!!....................well ive talked enough cant sleep hope all is well with u and family!............yall are so great I love yall muich! p.s. I no bens been talking to lily and all will you tell him I heard she was gonna sell pics of me.please ask him to ask her please don't that's why im so weird when it comes to people cause ive always gotten fucked for being so nice!...............wish u all the best, and hope to see u soon!................kiss

Anna was an enigma. No one could pin her down and make her do something she didn't want to do. You would think that, as a small-town hick, she would have been trampled on in court by J. Howard and E. Pierce Marshall's legal team, but over a decade later she outlived her rival, gained the help of the Supreme Court, and fought her case for millions with more determination than ever.

Even though she was taken to court on a regular basis, the law could only hold her back so much. Take her court case against Larry Birkhead, for example. She moved to the Bahamas and bought a house so that she could be a Bahamian resident and avoid American jurisdiction. Then, a California court ruled that she wasn't really a resident of the Bahamas because Anna had recently worked, lived and had a sexual relationship, with Birkhead, in California. However, despite the court order forcing her and Dannielynn to take a DNA test, Anna refused to comply and there was not much anyone could do about it.

What's funny is the recurring pattern with Anna. When J. Howard died she fought for his inheritance in the Texas courts. Then she claimed residency in California, filed for bankruptcy there, and started off an entirely separate court case from the one that was still pending in Texas. Then years later, when Larry Birkhead sued her in California, she claimed residency somewhere else to avoid the law.

I am surprised anyone could even get her to show up in court, considering the fact that she would do anything to get out of it. After Anna won the case against E. Pierce in the California courts, she dropped all charges against him in the Texas courts. She thought she had won millions of dollars without a fight and that would be it. She immediately booked a flight out of Texas, hoping to escape the state before their courts could subpoena her back.

However, E. Pierce was too quick for her. When she got to the airport, there was a barrage of fans awaiting her. They all wanted her autograph and she couldn't resist the attention. Little did she know that one of her "fans" was delivering her a court order. She signed her autograph on the papers that subpoenaed her back to court. She had been duped, and there was no way she could get out of it.

G. Ben Thompson had to sneak onto his own property in order to serve Anna, but the electric gates wouldn't open because he had cut off the power. He then sent his son-in-law to serve the eviction papers because there was no other way to get them to her.

Larry Birkhead had to wait for Anna and Howard to return to court in San Francisco before he could serve them with papers. Anna had been hiding out in the Bahamas making it impossible to reach her. However, once her case for J. Howard's millions continued, she was forced to make a pit stop in California in order to attend the hearing. Larry Birkhead had to quickly seize his chance before she disappeared again.

Anna had no qualms about breaking the law. As far as she was concerned, she was the law and what she said was all that mattered. It became a recurring theme that if anyone sued Anna, she would counter-sue with another claim. That is, if that person managed to trick Anna into court in the first place because serving my sister was like playing a role in *Mission: Impossible*. She disappeared the second you needed to find her.

REQUIEM

> *"Death is not the greatest loss in life.*
> *The greatest loss is what dies inside*
> *us while we live."*
> —NORMAN COUSINS

On February 5, 2007, Anna checked into the Seminole Hard Rock Hotel and Casino in Hollywood, Florida. She was there with Howard K. Stern and her bodyguard, Big Moe, to buy a yacht.

Prior to her departure from the Bahamas, Anna was ill with a high temperature that reached one-hundred-and-five degrees. She was given antiviral medicine that made her fever drop so she was able to fly. She was not getting any better in Florida and had to be bathed in ice water at the Hard Rock Hotel to cool her down.

On Thursday, February 7, 2007, Anna's nurse found her unconscious. The nurse called her husband, Big Moe, who was Anna's bodyguard and a trained paramedic, and told him that Anna was unresponsive. At 1:38 p.m., he called the hotel's front desk.

At about the same time, Anna's nurse began to administer CPR and a woman from the front desk called the Seminole police.

On the recording of that 911 call, which occurred at 1:42 p.m., the woman at the front desk could be heard calmly saying, "We need assistance to Room 607 at the Hard Rock. It's in reference to a white female. She's not breathing and not responsive...actually it's Anna Nicole Smith."

When Moe, arrived at Anna's room at 1.45 p.m., he took over from his wife and continued to administer CPR to Anna. According to Moe, he felt a flicker of a pulse and tried to resuscitate her. Just six minutes after the call to 911, a team of paramedics arrived on the scene. When they got to Anna's room, she was still unresponsive. The emergency crew left the hotel with Anna at 2:15 p.m. They reached Memorial Regional Hospital, located about three blocks from the hotel, six minutes later, at 2:21 p.m. On the way, they continued to perform CPR on Anna, but to no avail. At 2:49 p.m. Anna was pronounced dead on arrival.

Just under an hour after Anna died, a producer from the Fox News show *Hannity and Colmes* called me at my house. He said he didn't know if I had heard the news and he was very sorry to be the first to inform me. He told me my sister had been found unconscious on her hotel-room floor. There was a chance the paramedics wouldn't be able to resuscitate her. Again the producer told me how sorry he was that he had been the one to break the news to me. He understood that I needed time to digest the information but, if I were to talk publicly, he asked that I contact him first.

I thought it was a sick joke, another twist in Anna's life story. I called up my publicist, Karen Ammond, and asked her if there was any truth to his call. Karen could not yet confirm whether Anna was alive but, within minutes, Anna's death was the lead story around the world. It is devastating to hear someone dear to you is dead, but to find out through the media is even worse. This was the second death in my family I had found out about from a reporter. Five months earlier, I had been informed about Daniel's death by *The Insider* and *Entertainment Tonight*. With the relentless media attention around Anna's death, I sometimes imagine that it was staged to add more drama to her life. I still cannot believe it's real and that Anna is truly gone.

As a child, Anna told everyone, including me, she would be the next Marilyn Monroe. As an adult, she pursued her fantasy to the very end. Yet, Anna never quite made it. In the end, Anna died in Hollywood, but it was the wrong Hollywood. Anna was off by almost 3,000 miles. Marilyn Monroe died in Hollywood, California, not Hollywood, Florida.

From the moment her death was announced, questions were raised as to whether it was suicide, murder or an accident. Just as Marilyn Monroe's death launched all kinds of conspiracy theories, so too has Anna's death been grist for the tabloids and conspiracy theorists. With battles everywhere at the time of her death—the fight with J. Howard's heirs, the paternity fight over Dannielynn, lawsuits with TrimSpa, multiple lawsuits and claims over money and sex, and even an eerie after-death scandal involving the Bahamian immigration minister—there are more than enough would-be murderers for these theories.

Like her idol Marilyn Monroe, Anna wanted to be remembered as a legend and she will achieve her wish. In the end, the fights won't matter.

Everyone involved in the struggle over J. Howard's estate is now dead. I believe the Old Man's wealth was a curse for everyone it touched. J. Howard's passing was succeeded by his son, E. Pierce Marshall, and then by Anna's son Daniel, and finally, Anna herself. With all the key competitors out of the picture, only Anna's daughter and a phone book list of potential fathers were left to battle over the hypothetical inheritance.

Despite the façade she created, Anna was never happy. She had a history of drug addiction and had to depend on those around her for support. Anna always needed someone to lean on but, unfortunately, many of her friends were not trustworthy. Some were parasites. She married a cook, who she said abused her; a wheelchair-bound billionaire who used her; and then her lawyer, even after declaring publicly that she found him sexually repulsive. She needed someone on guard twenty-four-seven; if not her family, then a lover, husband or unwilling ex-boyfriend. She may have never personally paid a bill in her life, be it for electricity, lawyers, a coroner, or a roof over her head. She thought she was exempt from a conventional way of life and probably would not have known how to behave in any other manner.

It is not surprising Anna felt she was "trapped," and couldn't lead a normal life. She let Howard K. Stern sell the video of Dannielynn's caesarean delivery that he had shot, pictures of her and Daniel taken the day before he died, and her "commitment" ceremony with him. Just weeks later an interview with Anna about the death of her son was televised around the globe on *Entertainment Tonight*. My sister was living in her own self-inflicted prison with bars made out of money and drugs.

After Daniel died, Anna led a life of depression. She was condemned by the media for her role as a mother, marriage to Howard K. Stern, and history of drug abuse. All the while, she continued the ten-year fight for her late husband, J. Howard's, estate. The only light in her life was her newborn daughter, Dannielynn, and, as Big Moe stated, it was barely surprising that she died while Dannielynn was in the Bahamas, away from Anna.

As Anna's sister, I knew her life was spiraling out of control months before she died. If only Anna could have talked to me. But, at the end, Howard K. Stern succeeded in pushing me and all of Anna's family from her life. The only way I could communicate with Anna was through the media, and I did. On *A Current Affair* and *Entertainment Tonight*, just months before her death, I told Anna she needed to be aware of the people around her and I feared the harm she was doing to herself was going to kill her.

Virgie also reached out. Again, sadly, through the media. She told Anna, with ominous accuracy, that if she continued with her ways she would end up like her son, Daniel. On October 12, 2006, Virgie told Nancy Grace on CNN, "Vickie Lynn, you know I love you, always have. And be very careful about who you hang around with, because you may be next."

In December 2006, Virgie said on *The Dr. Keith Ablow Show*, "I'm disappointed that she got mixed up in drugs and the wrong people...she lives on drugs now." She directed her words at Anna, saying: "Vickie Lynn, please, you have a family baby...we're still here for you. You don't have to have drugs, you've got a beautiful baby girl now. You need to start life over, you need to be a great mom and live life now."

Instead of listening to her family's advice, Anna took our public pleas as personal attacks and lashed out at those who truly loved her. Perhaps it was wrong of us to communicate with Anna through the media, but there was no other way to get through to her. Anna would not talk to us and she had a team to protect her from any external forces.

In my eyes, Anna wasn't living for months before she died. After the loss of her beloved son, she couldn't take the pain anymore and whether intentionally or recklessly, put an end to her life of misery. Daniel was the only person Anna knew she could trust. From the time she took him back from Virgie's care, Anna and her son were inseparable. When Daniel died, it was as if Anna had been robbed of her soul.

PAGES FROM ANNA'S
DIARY IN 1992 AND 1994.

DAY Wensday   DATE 6-3-92
Went to mall today caught myself looking at baby stuff I hope I'm not pregnant I havent started my period. I worried about it. I dont no what I will do if I am. Al will only support me if I have it but if I Decide to go the other way he wont I'll be on my own. I think thats tackie, I'm scared

DAY Thursday   DATE 6-4-92
Well I had a very exciting day!! I told Clay we would just be friends. Al came over and stayed the nite. Then Clay came over at 2:00 am And was banging on the window so Al called the police + was so scared!! :(Dont no whats gonna happen now Bye Bye

DAY Wends   DATE 6-17-92
Ate lunch with Howard Then did playmate hotline then went to promotion at Byou Mamas took mom we had a blast I twas so much fun Bill was there everybody went crazy when I went on stage It felt so good. But me and mom got so drunk felt like shit this mourning.

Anna writes that she was pregnant in 1992 and she was having an affair with Clay Spires and Alex Bolt while she was dating J. Howard Marshall.

Anna had a very close relationship with her mother, Virgie, while J. Howard Marshall was alive.

DAY _Tuesday_ DATE 7-14th-92

I'm sick got a Summer cold. it sucks, Going to Lot farm 16th then New York 21st, Takin Dammy to Dentist tomorrow,

DAY _Monday_ DATE 8-16-92

Well I'm going to Miami for my 1st real shoot for Guess. I'm kinda scared I'm afraid Paul will find out about my past and be so upset and fire me and not want to see me, anymore. But I just cant tell him. I'm ashamed. I've been really stressed out lately and depressed and I cant quit eating. I feel like a pig. Howard has been buying me some jewlry. But he call me 15 or 20 times a day it drives me crazy. I love him but he agravates me somtimes I don't no what to do about Paul hes strange guy. I hate for men to want sex all the time. I hate sex anyway I only like it with Clay now that hes out of my life. I hate sex. Well I best be going to sleep now. I'm tired and got a big day tomorrow. Chow Daniel starts school the 24th but I'll be in Miami I wish I could be here for his 1st Day of school.

Chow!

Anna was always worried that Paul Marciano would end her 3-year multi-million dollar Guess? contract, which he had the right to do if Anna harmed the clothing line's image in any way.

There is no doubt that Anna loved J. Howard and the support he offered her. Sadly, she could not remain faithful to him.

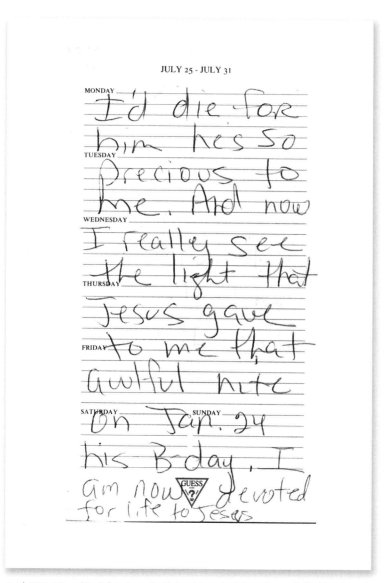

In July 1994, J. Howard Marshall was in poor health. Anna felt very lonely during this period of her life and turned to Jesus for help.

EPILOGUE

Well, I promised you that I would tell you what I know about my sister, and what I suspect based on what I've seen, who I know and who I believe. I don't think I got anything wrong, but if I did and someone can prove that to me, I'll change my opinion and be the first to say I'm sorry. It's just my opinion, but I've come to realize that I'm good at reading people and situations and deciding who to trust.

Finally, my sister Vickie Lynn Hogan, who was known to the world as Anna Nicole Smith, can finally rest in peace in the Bahamas beside the true love of her life, her son, Daniel Wayne Smith. Goodbye. I love you.

To My Sister Anna

That you are gone is harder than I thought it could be. I know we have been estranged for ten years, how now I wish we had those years back. The day you passed away started as a typical day for me. I made sure the kids got off to school, worked on my business and fed the dogs. Then Fox News called me and asked me if I'd heard the news about my sister. The producer told me that Vickie had been found unconscious at the Hard Rock Café.

My first reaction was that you had a relapse of pneumonia. But then I called my friend Karen who told me she feared it could be worse than that. She waited on the line with me until she had confirmation from a friend of hers who works at CNN. The worst had happened. She said she was sorry. Without her saying more, I knew what she meant.

My heart sank and I shook. This can't be true, I said to her. But, Karen replied, it was true. She then said the words. She said you were really gone. I immediately flashed back to scenes of us separated as little girls. Our daddy would drive me by your house and I would see you in pigtails swinging so happily on your swing set.

I remember how proud I was when you became the Guess? Jeans model and your fame began to build. I remember what you said to me, that you had done what you promised all of us you would do, make a better life for yourself and Daniel. I remember those many conversations we had when I was pregnant and how you said you hoped I had a girl just as you had always dreamed of having your own daughter one day. You were one of the most beautiful women in the world.

My dear sister, you were a wonderful mother to Daniel. I never in my days ever saw a mother and son as close as you both were. I know you are together in heaven.

I am angry that you were taken away this early. I am angry that the people around you did not protect you. I am angry that they shoved your family away. We needed you and you needed us. We both said things in anger over the last few years. It wasn't easy for me to deal with this rejection. It was so confusing. But now I understand better why certain people did not want your family in your life. They wanted to control you and we would have been in the way. Vickie, we never wanted a dime from you. All we ever wanted is the same thing we had to offer, love.

There were times I was embarrassed by your actions in the public eye. Now, I think about it and I realize those actions probably were caused by the prescription medications you were on. You were in pain, emotionally and physically, and no one was helping you! Why??

There were times I was embarrassed by your actions in the public eye. Now, I think about it and I realize those actions were probably caused by the prescription medications you were on. You were in pain, emotionally and physically, and no one was helping you! Why?

Howard K. Stern was with you practically every minute of the day for the last five months of your life. He acted as your manager, publicist, attorney, friend and common law husband. He lived off you and, according to him, you were his everything. However, from all the recent reports and testimonies in court about your move to the Bahamas, the drugs you were taking, your many aliases and your relationship with Howard, it is very hard to believe he was not responsible for your death. He must have known you were mixing methadone with other drugs, and there is a picture showing him collecting drugs for you. It is obvious to me that not only did he fail to stop you from destroying yourself, he was actually an enabler who led you astray and caused your death.

I started this book last year. 2006 started as a good year for you, and ended so sadly with Daniel's passing. In writing this book, I hoped we could both place all our cards on the table and come back together. I was hoping that we could learn to cope with our history and again be a family. I really thought that we could overcome those who stood in our way. Now, I have forever lost that chance. I never got to tell you how much I love you. I never got to say goodbye.

The media and public don't understand who we really are, or who you really were. They just print what they want. I know you loved me as I did you. My promise to you and to Daniel is that I make sure that Dannielynn Hope will know she has family who loves her and who will protect her forever.

We do not want one cent from any inheritance or estate. What we want is to make sure Dannielynn knows we will watch out for her and love her forever. She must stay safe from bad people and NOT be a pawn for money.

I miss you. Rest in peace, Vickie Lynn Hogan.

Your baby sister

Donna

ACKNOWLEDGEMENTS

I'd like to devote this book to my wonderful, beautiful children, who are my pride and joy. I was blessed by God to have been given each one and I can't imagine life without them. To my close friend and confidante, April, I can't say enough about her friendship and what it has meant to me, she is my substitute sister. To Karen Ammond my publicist and dear friend who not only offered me countless hours helping me with the media, but also emotional support and her friendship, I offer my thanks and love. If not for her kindness, I would still be wallowing in misery.

My thanks and love also to my cousin Cynthia, who is the best photographer in Texas. She spent time to photograph me for this book and for that I thank her! Of course, my thanks for all the wonderful support I have received from my close family friends. Your friendship and support means so very much to me and you will always be in my heart.

To Michael Viner for publishing my story, I am forever grateful and to Henrietta Tiefenthaler, without whom I could not have written this book, you are the greatest.

DONNA HOGAN

I would also like to thank Phoenix Books' publisher Michael Viner and chairman Kenin M. Spivak for publishing this remarkable story. We started on this book long before Anna's tragic death. Despite any speculation to the contrary, except for the sad duty of changing the tenses, a few revisions and the last chapter, the manuscript was completed before Anna passed away.

Thank you also to Kenin Spivak for editing the book; Creighton Vero for his invaluable insights; Francine Uyetake and Margie Nunan for their comments; and my mother, father, and sister for their moral support.

Henrietta Tiefenthaler

The
Anna Nicole Smith
Family Tree

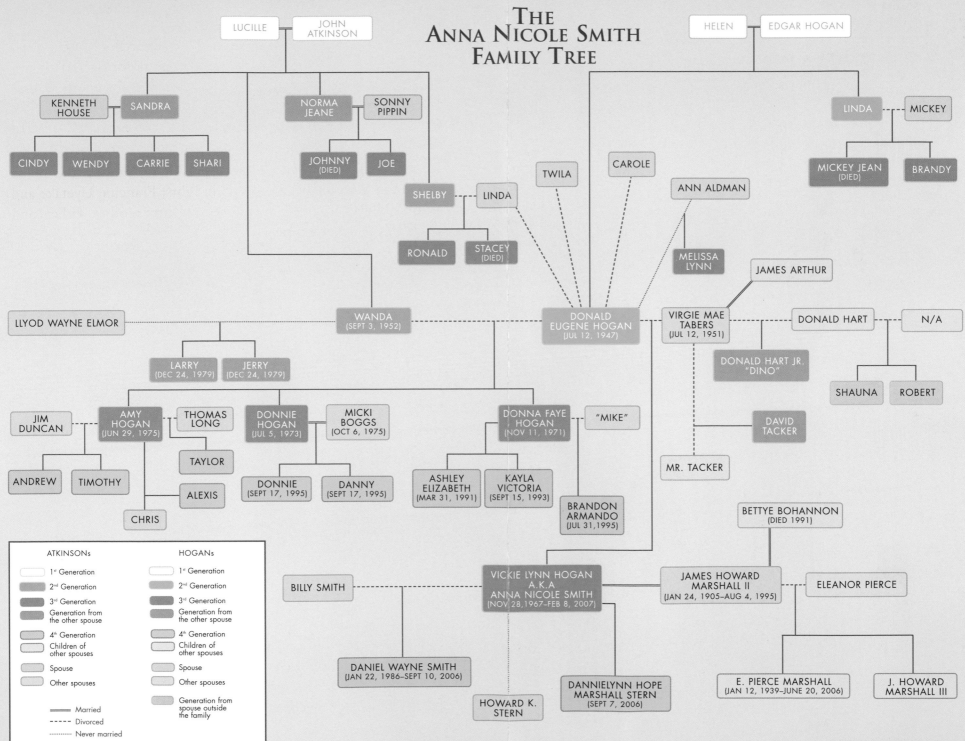